ANTHOLOGY OF

Twentieth-Century Music

ANTHOLOGY OF

Twentieth-Century Music

MARY H. WENNERSTROM

Indiana University

PRENTICE-HALL, INC.

Englewood Cliffs, New Jersey

Printed in the United States of America

ISBN: 0-13-038489-5

Library of Congress Catalog Card Number: 79-80886

10 9 8 7 6 5 4

PRENTICE-HALL INTERNATIONAL, INC., *London*
PRENTICE-HALL OF AUSTRALIA, PTY. LTD., *Sydney*
PRENTICE-HALL OF CANADA, LTD., *Toronto*
PRENTICE-HALL OF INDIA PRIVATE LIMITED, *New Delhi*
PRENTICE-HALL OF JAPAN, INC., *Tokyo*

ACKNOWLEDGEMENTS

Béla Bartók, *Mikrokosmos No. 46, Increasing-Diminishing; No. 126, Change of Time;* and *No. 148, Six Dances in Bulgarian Rhythm, No. 1* from MIKROKOSMOS. Copyright 1940 in U. S. A. by Hawkes & Son (London), Ltd. Copyright for all countries. Reprinted with permission of Boosey and Hawkes, Inc., New York.

Béla Bartók, *Violin Duet No. 33, Song of the Harvest* from FORTY-FOUR VIOLIN DUETS. Copyright 1933 by Universal Edition. Copyright assigned 1939 to Hawkes & Son (London), Ltd., for the British Empire, U. S. A., and all countries of South and Central America. Reprinted with permission of Boosey and Hawkes, Inc., New York.

Béla Bartók, First movement from SIXTH QUARTET. Copyright 1941 in U. S. A. by Hawkes & Son (London), Ltd. Copyright for all countries. Reprinted with permission of Boosey and Hawkes, Inc., New York.

Alban Berg, *Songs Op. 2, No. 3* and *No. 4* from FOUR SONGS, OP. 2. Copyright 1928 by Schlesinger'sche Buch-u. Musikhdl., Berlin-Lichterfelde. Copyright renewal 1956 by Frau Helene Berg, Vienna. Reprinted by permission of Theodore Presser Co., Bryn Mawr, Pennsylvania.

Alban Berg, *Marie's Lullaby* from WOZZECK. Full score copyright 1926 by Universal Edition, A. G., Vienna. Full score copyright renewed 1954 by Helene Berg. Reprinted by permission of Theodore Presser Co., Bryn Mawr, Pennsylvania.

Elliott Carter, *Etude No. 7* and *Fantasy* (excerpt) from EIGHT ETUDES AND A FANTASY FOR WOODWIND QUARTET. Copyright © 1955, 1959 by Associated Music Publishers, Inc. Reprinted by permission of Associated Music Publishers, Inc., New York.

Aaron Copland, excerpt from APPALACHIAN SPRING. Copyright 1945 in U. S. A. by Hawkes & Son (London), Ltd. Copyright for all countries. Reprinted by permission of Boosey and Hawkes, Inc., New York.

Kenneth Gaburo, ANTIPHONY IV. Copyright © 1967 by Kenneth Gaburo. Permission to reproduce this score has been given by the composer.

Paul Hindemith, Second movement (excerpt) from STRING QUARTET, OP. 22. Copyright by B. Schott's Sohne, Mainz, 1923. Copyright renewed by Schott and Co., Ltd., London, 1951. Reprinted by permission of Associated Music Publishers, Inc., New York.

Paul Hindemith, *Interlude* and *Fugue in A* from LUDUS TONALIS. Copyright 1943 by Associated Music Publishers, Inc., New York. Copyright 1943 by Schott and Co., Ltd., London. Reprinted by permission of Associated Music Publishers, Inc., New York.

Charles Ives, Third movement, *The Revival* from SECOND SONATA FOR VIOLIN AND PIANO. Copyright 1951 by G. Schirmer, Inc., New York. Used by permission.

Vincent Persichetti, Sixth movement, *March* from DIVERTIMENTO FOR BAND. Copyright 1951 by Oliver Ditson Co. Used by permission.

Mel Powell, excerpt from FILIGREE SETTING FOR STRING QUARTET. Copyright © 1965 by G. Schirmer, Inc., New York. International copyright secured. Used by permission.

Arnold Schoenberg, Piano piece *Op. 19, No. 2* from SIX SHORT PIECES FOR PIANO, OP. 19. Copyright 1915 by Universal Edition. Renewed copyright 1940 by Arnold Schoenberg. Used by permission of Belmont Music Publishers, Los Angeles, California 90049 and Universal Edition, A. G., Vienna.

Arnold Schoenberg, *Gavotte* and *Musette* from SUITE FOR PIANO, OP. 25. Copyright 1925 by Universal Edition. Copyright renewed 1952 by Gertrude Schoenberg. Used by permission of Belmont Music Publishers, Los Angeles, California 90049 and Universal Edition, A. G., Vienna.

Arnold Schoenberg, *Introduction, Theme,* and *Variation I* from VARIATIONS FOR ORCHESTRA, OP. 31. Copyright 1929 by Universal Edition. Copyright renewed 1956 by Gertrude Schoenberg. Used by permission of Belmont Music Publishers, Los Angeles, California 90049 and Universal Edition, A. G., Vienna.

Gunther Schuller, III, *Little Blue Devil* from SEVEN STUDIES ON THEMES OF PAUL KLEE. Copyright © 1962 by Universal Edition (London), Ltd. Used by permission of Theodore Presser Co., Bryn Mawr, Pennsylvania.

Igor Stravinsky, *Russian Dance* from PETROUSHKA. Reprinted by permission of Boosey and Hawkes, Inc., New York.

Igor Stravinsky, *The Soldier's March, Great Chorale,* and *Triumphal March of the Devil* from L'HISTOIRE DU SOLDAT. Reprinted by permission of J. & W. Chester Ltd., London.

Igor Stravinsky, *Dirge-Canons* (*Prelude*) from IN MEMORIAM DYLAN THOMAS. Copyright 1954 by Boosey and Hawkes, Inc., New York. Used by permission of Boosey and Hawkes, Inc., New York.

Igor Stravinsky, II, *Surge, aquilo* from CANTICUM SACRUM. Copyright © 1956 by Boosey and Hawkes, Inc., New York. Used by permission of Boosey and Hawkes, Inc., New York.

Anton Webern, Orchestra piece *Op. 6 No. 1* from SIX PIECES FOR ORCHESTRA, OP. 6. Copyright © 1956 by Universal Edition, A. G., Vienna. Used by permission of Theodore Presser Co., Bryn Mawr, Pennsylvania.

Anton Webern, First movement from CANTATA, OP. 29. Copyright © 1957 by Universal Edition. A. G., Vienna. Used by permission of Theodore Presser Co., Bryn Mawr, Pennsylvania.

Preface

The twentieth century is more than two-thirds over, yet the music of this century is often regarded as too difficult to understand or perform. Twentieth-century music, with its sometimes bewildering diversity of styles, does demand, in many instances, a new approach in analysis and performance, although in much music traditional elements are only covered by a layer of new sounds or techniques. The purpose of this anthology is to present a limited group of twentieth-century compositions to the student and teacher for use in theory and literature courses or for private study. There is no current anthology which is devoted completely to twentieth-century music, and this collection hopes to fill a part of the need for available contemporary material.

Several criteria guided the selection of material. First, only complete pieces, movements, or long excerpts are used; a real understanding of the structure and shape of twentieth-century music demands that isolated materials (chords, melodies, etc.) be placed in context. Second, only recorded compositions are included, as it is useful to make the sound of the music available to those who are unable to perform all of the pieces. Third, the composers are important figures in twentieth-century music and the compositions demonstrate interesting facets of twentieth-century style.

In the selection of compositions, it soon became obvious that the anthology could not possibly include all "schools" and styles of the twentieth century. Several "staple" composers were selected as a nucleus (Schoenberg, Berg, Webern, Stravinsky, Bartók, and Hindemith) and then several American composers were chosen to represent diverse trends (Carter, Copland, Gaburo, Ives, Persichetti, Powell, and Schuller). This list is by no means complete and it is hoped that the reader will supplement these compositions by study of many other twentieth-century composers, from all countries. However, the American composers selected represent American music (and in many ways European music) from the Ives of 1908 to the Gaburo of 1967. The United States is now perhaps in a position to lead musically rather than to follow. Certainly the current trends of involved serial composition, aleatoric music, combinations of sound with other stimuli, and electronic and computer music are all evident on the American scene, and some of these trends, as well as earlier ideas, are reflected in the anthology.

The use of the book is left to the student and teacher. It can be adapted to analysis classes, to literature and history classes, and to individual projects. For each composition there is a short text, which deals briefly with a biography of the composer and historical information about the piece. The questions are designed to direct the student's attention to important elements in the composition; they should be regarded as the springboard for a thorough analysis and discussion. The student is also encouraged to compare pieces in the anthology, to study the complete scores of the works, and to study other compositions of a similar nature. It is hoped that a study of the compositions in the anthology will lead to a fuller appreciation of twentieth-century music and will equip the reader with skills to approach and understand a wide range of music.

Translations are given where necessary for the vocal works. Piano reductions are given with the more complex scores to facilitate analysis and to provide a simpler means of performing the score. In some cases a reduction was not attempted, as it seemed that the sounds of the original could not be duplicated on the piano. In other places the complexity of the score demanded a two-piano or a one piano, four hand reduction. These reductions should not be regarded as performing versions but as aids for studying and understanding the music.

Following the music are lists of the selections arranged chronologically and by medium. A selected list of current recordings of the compositions is also included.

One of the main considerations delaying an anthology of twentieth-century music is the copyright permission problem. Longer excerpts from some composers simply cannot be reprinted. I was aware of this difficulty when beginning the project and have spent considerable effort to overcome this barrier. However, in general the publishers contacted have been helpful and generous, and I would like to express my sincere thanks to all the copyright holders who have allowed these compositions to be reprinted.

I would like also to acknowledge the many people who have contributed to this project, especially students and colleagues in the theory department at Indiana University. Especially I would like to thank Dr. R. P. DeLone and Dr. Vernon Kliewer for their ideas and encouragement, Mr. Peter Alexander for assistance in the preparation of the manuscript, and Mr. Robert Spencer, music editor of Appleton-Century-Crofts, for his many solutions to problems which arose. Hopefully this anthology will be a useful addition to the study and understanding of twentieth-century music.

M.H.W.

Contents

BÉLA BARTÓK

1881, Nagyszentmiklós, Hungary—1945, New York

Bartók was an Hungarian musician, trained in Budapest, who was intensely interested in his native folk music. In collaboration with Zoltán Kodály, Bartók did much scholarly research on ethnic Slovak music. He was also a talented pianist and a prolific composer.

In his pedagogical collections of music, Bartók presented contemporary materials and techniques in a systematic manner. His larger works have a tightness of construction and an exciting and convincing melodic and rhythmic development; these works place Bartók among the great composers of the first half of the twentieth century.

MIKROKOSMOS, 1926-1937

The *Mikrokosmos* are 153 progressive piano pieces arranged in six volumes. In addition to teaching piano technique, the pieces are a complete, compressed exposition of twentieth-century materials and structure and are musical entities in their own right. Most of the pieces deal with one primary element, which is described in their titles. Three pieces are reproduced here, ranging from the simple to the complex.

No. 46, Vol. II., Increasing-Diminishing

1. List all the elements which are "increasing and diminishing." How do they contribute to form?
2. Discuss the pitch material of this piece (scale basis, tonal center).

BÉLA BARTÓK

Mikrokosmos

NO. 46, INCREASING—DIMINISHING

No. 126, Vol. V., Change of Time

1. What creates phrasing in this piece?
2. What is the unit of pulse? How is the pulse grouped into metric patterns?
3. Compare rhythm and meter here to the rhythm and meter in Stravinsky's "Triumphal March of the Devil" from *L'Histoire du Soldat,* reproduced in this anthology.
4. What kinds of sonorities are used? Compare harmonizations of repeated melodic units.
5. How is tonality established? Compare pitch centers of the melody with pitch centers of harmonic progressions.

NO. 126, CHANGE OF TIME

No. 148, Vol. VI., Six Dances in Bulgarian Rhythm, No. 1

1. Why is the meter signature not $\frac{9}{8}$? Enumerate the basic rhythmic patterns of the composition.
2. What is the tonal center? How is it established? What kinds of scales are used?
3. How does Bartók treat the original melodic idea (measures 4-8)? What kind of form results from this treatment?
4. Compare the melodic line to that of Stravinsky's *Petroushka,* "Russian Dance." Compare the two dances as to formal construction, rhythm, national characteristics, and dance qualities.

NO. 148, SIX DANCES IN BULGARIAN RHYTHM, NO. 1.

più f
15
20
mf
mp
25
p
8

espr.
30
rit. - - - al -
mf
Meno vivo, ♪ = 240
poco a poco accelerando - - -
35
p cresc. - - -
(Ped.)
al
f
Tempo I.
40
sempre f
mf

poco allarg.
f
più f
Calmo
45
mf
mf
p
p
rinf.
tornando al
50
p dolce
p
più p
mf
Tempo I.
f
55
sempre f
marc.
poco rit.
Tempo I.
ff
60
sff
[1 min. 50 sec.]

Bartók, FORTY-FOUR VIOLIN DUETS, 1931

This collection is another graded one, progressing from simple to complex works for two violins. As in the *Mikrokosmos,* Bartók explores a range of contemporary materials, here combined with a variety of violin techniques.

No. 33, Song of the Harvest

1. Analyze the pitch material. Are there any tonal centers or consistent scale patterns?
2. How is the piece divided into sections?
3. Study the counterpoint. What relationships exist between the two lines? Compare measures 1-5 and measures 16-20.

BÉLA BARTÓK

Forty-four Violin Duets

NO. 33, SONG OF THE HARVEST

Bartók, SIXTH QUARTET, 1939

The sixth is the last of the group of Bartók string quartets, compositions which hold a major place in twentieth-century music. The first movement, reproduced here (*Mesto; Vivace*), exposes the basic material of the quartet. It is especially interesting to trace the opening *Mesto* viola solo through the *mesto* sections that open each succeeding movement; this solo develops into a complete last movement. The sad, pensive opening provides a consistent melodic and emotional thread throughout the quartet. The quartet is dedicated to the Kolisch Quartet.

First Movement, Mesto; Vivace

1. Analyze the opening viola solo for melodic intervals, motives, and phrase construction. Listen to the complete quartet and trace this opening solo throughout the four movements.
2. Listen to the first movement. Sketch out the form of the movement and enumerate several elements that create form.
3. Write out the important melodic material of the first movement. Study this material in detail for interval construction and rhythmic motives. Trace the melodic and rhythmic patterns through the movement and list developmental processes that Bartók employs.
4. Compare the opening solo to the melodic material and processes used in the main body of the first movement. Are there similarities of interval patterns, melodic construction, or melodic development?
5. Analyze the texture of the movement, studying such things as spacing, doubling, placement of melodic material, and relationships of the four voices. Select sections (*e.g.*, measures 81-98 or measures 180-193) for detailed study.
6. Discuss the pitch material of the movement. What intervals are important? What kinds of chords are used? Are there melodic or harmonic tonal centers?
7. Compare this string quartet to other string compositions in this anthology and to such works as Debussy *String Quartet*, Schoenberg *Fourth String Quartet*, and Berg *Lyric Suite*.

OTHER WORKS TO STUDY

Bartók, Béla:
String Quartet, No. 1 (1910)
Suite for Piano, Op. 14 (1916)
String Quartet, No. 4 (1928)
Music for Strings, Percussion, and Celesta, I (1935)
Sonata for Two Pianos and Percussion, I (1937)
Concerto for Orchestra, I and II (1943)

BÉLA BARTÓK

Sixth Quartet

FIRST MOVEMENT

31
36
41
47
gliss.
gliss.
gliss.
pizz.
arco
pizz.
arco
pizz.
arco
cresc.
dim.

53
p cresc. molto
f
p
f
cresc. molto
f, in rilievo
f
60
sf
p
sf
p
cresc.
f
mf
f
mp
sf
cresc.
sf
p
cresc.
68
marcato
sempre sim.
f
mf
mf
mf
f
mf
76
dim.
dim
marc.
sempre sim.
dim.
dim.

poco a poco rall. - - - - - - al - -
81
Un poco meno vivo, ♩. = ca. 120
p, ma con calore
p
p
55''
p
pizz.
p, grazioso
(sim.)
89
p, leggero, in ril.
poco - a - poco -
f
f
in ril.
f sub.
f sub.
p
- tornando - - - - - - - - al - - - - - -
Vivacissimo, agitato, ♩. = 160
99
p
f
f
p
ff
p sub.
p sub.
p sub.
f in ril.
mf
f in ril.
17''
p sub.

cresc.
109
f
p
III
117
Ancora più vivo, 𝅗𝅥. = 176
mp
mf

126
137
Tempo I. (♩. = 140)
cresc.
27"
144

150
un poco rall.
pp
pp
II
pp
pp
20"
158
Pesante, ♩. = 120
(lunga)
f
ff
166
Tempo I. (♩. = 140)
IV
pizz.
sempre ff
mf

174
arco
arco
(lunga
27
180
186
194
pizz.

201
p
sf
mf
dim.
pizz.
p
209
sf
p
arco
mf
217

222
cresc.
arco
34"
sim.
231
sempre ff
237
p
mp
pp
5

242
p
mp
247
mp
mp
256
pp
pp
pp
pp
poco cresc.
poco cresc.
poco cresc.
poco cresc.
262
dim.
dim.
dim.
dim.

poco rall.
Un poco tranquillo, ♩. = ca.120
268
pp
p, dolce
88"
p
(lunga) Vivacissimo, ♩. = ca. 160-150
276
282
tornando
287
al
Tempo I. (♩. = 140)
mp

un poco rallent.
(lunga)
Vivacissimo, 𝅗𝅥. = ca. 160
297
pp
pp
pp
pp
p
pp
308
cresc.
cresc.
cresc.
cresc.
pp
rallent.
al-
f
dim.
f
dim.
-p
f
dim.
-p
f
dim.
pp
pp
pp
40"
312
Meno vivo, 𝅗𝅥. = ca. 120
p
mf
mf
p
mf
p
f, in ril.

320
cresc.
f
più f
ff
un poco
allarg.
332
Vivacissimo, agitato, ♩. = ca. 160
p sub.
19"
♩. = 150
342
cresc.
sf

(lunga)
rallent. - - - a tempo (Tempo I., ♩. = 140)
355
p, dolce
dolce
19''
poco - - - a - -poco - rallent. - - -
368
(arco)
pizz.
pizz.
pizz.
(arco)
♩. = 120
arco

371
a tempo (♩. = 140)
poco rall. - - - a tempo, ma tranquillo,
♩. = ca. 180
pizz.
arco
pizz.
arco
881
poco a poco rallent. - - -
dim. -
dim. -
dim. -
dim. -
Lento, ♩. = 90
pp
pp
pp
pp
40"
(Durée 6'46")

ALBAN BERG

1885, Vienna—1935, Vienna

Alban Berg, an Austrian composer, met Arnold Schoenberg in 1904 and became his pupil and intimate friend. Berg's music is rooted in the late nineteenth-century German romantic tradition and demonstrates a sense of order combined with dramatic climax and contrast. Berg's later works illustrate a rather loose application of Schoenberg's twelve-tone system. None of the excerpts reproduced here are serial; each illustrates a free approach to tonality combined with traditional harmonic elements.

FOUR SONGS, Op. 2, 1908-1909

These four songs were written while Berg was still a student of Schoenberg. They use texts by Hebbel, a nineteenth-century German poet, and by Mombert, one of Berg's contemporaries. The songs are an extension of the musical ideas of Mahler, Wolf, and Strauss, but Numbers 3 and 4, reproduced here, show the transition from traditional tonality to a much freer concept of tonal organization. The songs indicate the dramatic and expressionistic direction that Berg was to follow in his operatic works. These songs, originally written with piano accompaniment, have been orchestrated for voice and chamber orchestra by René Leibowitz.

Op. 2, No. 3

Nun ich der Riesen Stärksten überwand,	I overcame the strongest of giants
Mich aus dem dunkelsten Land heimfand,	And found my way home from the darkest land,
An einer weissen Märchenhand,	Led by a white fairy hand,
Hallen schwer die Glokken;	Heavily the bells chime;
Und ich wanke durch die Gassen schlafbefangen.	And I falter through the alleys overcome by sleep.

Alfred Mombert, from *Der Glühende* (1896)

1. Discuss the melodic unifying factors in the piano part and the voice line.
2. Analyze this song using traditional tonal and harmonic functional analysis. What similarities are there to a traditional major or minor tonality? Consider sonorities, harmonic progressions, cadences, and tonal centers. Of what significance is the key signature?
3. What sort of form is created in the song? Study melodic and harmonic returns, repetitions, and contrasts.

ALBAN BERG

Four Songs, Op. 2

NO. 3

*) *Diese Stellen nicht hastig, sondern im Tempo des gesprochenen Wortes.*

Berg, Op. 2, No. 4

Warm die Lüfte, es spriesst Gras auf sonnigen Wiesen,
Horch! Horch, es flötet die Nachtigall.
Ich will singen:
Droben hoch im düstern Bergforst,
Es schmilzt und glitzert kalter Schnee,
Ein Mädchen in grauem Kleide lehnt an feuchtem Eichstamm,
Krank sind ihre zarten Wangen,
Die grauen Augen fiebern durch Düsterriesen-stämme.
„Er kommt noch nicht. Er lässt mich warten."
Stirb! Der Eine stirbt, daneben der Andre lebt:
Das macht die Welt so tiefschön.

Warm the breezes, there is grass in sunny meadows,
Hark! Hark, the nightingale is singing.
I want to sing:
High over in the somber mountain wood,
The cold snow melts and glistens,
A maiden dressed in grey leans against the moist oak,
Sick are her fragile cheeks,
Her grey eyes feverishly peering through gloomy giant trunks.
"He does not come. He leaves me waiting!"
Die! The one dies, close by the other lives:
This makes the world so deeply beautiful.

Alfred Mombert, from *Der Glühende* (1896)

1. What creates form (*i.e.,* unity and contrast) in this song? What sort of shape does this piece have? Consider the text and emotional-dramatic factors as well as musical elements.
2. What kinds of sonorities, progressions, and cadences are used in this song? Compare Op. 2, No. 4 to Op. 2, No. 3 as to harmonic and tonal elements.
3. Study the vocal line for intervals used, range, melodic patterns, and text setting. How does it compare to the other vocal pieces in the anthology?
4. How are the sound and expressionistic possibilities of the piano used?
5. Compare these two Berg songs to Schoenberg's Op. 19, No. 2 and to Webern's Op. 6, No. 1, both reproduced in the anthology.

OP. 2, NO. 4

*) Der Vorschlag ruhig und langsam zu nehmen!

accel.
rit.
Eich-stamm, krank sind ih-re zar-ten Wan - gen, die grau-en Au-gen fie - bern durch
15
accel. rit.
Dü-ster-rie-sen-stäm - me.
ff
„Er kommt noch nicht.
gliss.
molto
sffz
Rit. Accel.
molto
fff
Er läßt mich war - ten..."
Rit. Accel.
molto sffz
sffz
Rit. Accel.
ff martellato
(tonlos)
Stirb!
20
p
Der Ei-ne
l.H. r.H.
molto rit. ganz langsam
fff
p dolce
sehr ruhig
kurzer Halt.
p
stirbt, da-ne-ben der An-dre lebt: Das macht die Welt so tief - schön.
25
espress. mp
p
pp
ppp

Berg, WOZZECK, 1921

Wozzeck is one of the important operas of the twentieth century. Based on a drama of 1836 by Georg Büchner, the story centers around the soldier Wozzeck—a man imprisoned by his society and by his own lonely tragedy. Berg's opera is a cohesive and effective dramatic and musical work. *Wozzeck* was first performed in 1925.

The opera is structured musically into three acts, which are three musical forms: five character sketches (Act I), a symphony in five movements (Act II), and five variations (Act III). Act I, Scene 3 is a sketch of Marie, Wozzeck's mistress. Near the beginning of this scene she sings of herself and her child in the excerpt reproduced here.

WOZZECK, Marie's Lullaby

Mädel, was fangst Du jetst an?
Hast ein klein Kind und kein Mann!
Ei, was frag'ich darnach,
Sing' ich die ganze Nacht:
Eia popeia, mein süsser Bu',
Gibt mir kein Mensch nix dazu!

Hansel, spann' Deine sechs Schimmel an,
Gib sie zu fressen auf's neu.
Kein Haber fresse sie,
Kein Wasser saufe sie,
Lauter kühle Wein muss es sein!
Lauter kühle Wein muss es sein!

Maiden, what song shall you sing?
You have a child, but no ring!
Why such sorrow pursue?
Singing the whole night through:
Hushabye baby, my darling son,
Nobody cares, ne'er a one.

Jackie, go saddle your horses now,
Give them to eat and to spare.
No oats to eat today,
No water drink today,
Purest, coolest wine shall it be!
Purest, coolest wine shall it be!

Translated by Eric Blackall and Vida Harford

1. Listen to the first three scenes of the opera.
2. Analyze the vocal line of this excerpt. What sort of rhythmic and melodic patterns are used?
3. Analyze chord construction. How do the sonority types used compare to the melodic patterns of the vocal line?
4. Sketch the form of this excerpt. What creates phrases and sections in this piece?
5. Listen to as much of the opera as possible (especially Act III). Notice reminiscences of the lullaby (*e.g.*, Act III, Scene 5) and notate other melodic patterns that return.

OTHER WORKS TO STUDY

Berg, Alban: *Wozzeck*, Act III, Scenes 1 and 2
Lyric Suite (1926)
Concerto for Violin and Orchestra (1935)

ALBAN BERG

Wozzeck

MARIE'S LULLABY

375
rit. - - - molto rit.
1. Ob.
Bkl. in B
1. Fg.
1. Hr. in F o. D. 2.
Hfe
Marie
Mann! Ei, was frag'ich dar - nach, Sing' ich die gan - ze Nacht:
ring. Why such sor - row pur - sue? Sing ing the whole night through;
375
rit. - - - molto rit.
1. Solo m. D.
1. Vl.
2. Solo m. D.
1. Vl.
d. Übrig. o. D.
o. Dpf.
arco
m. Dpf.
1. Solo m. D.
Vla
2. Solo m. D.
(m. Dpf.)
d. Übrig. o. D.
1. Solo m. D.
Vlc.
2. Solo m. D.
Vlc.
3. Solo m. D.
375
rit. - - - molto rit.

Bedeutend langsamer (Tempo II) (♩ = ca 72-80)
Die neuen ♩ entsprechen den letzten ♪ des rit.
380
1. Fl.
2. Hr. in F o. D.
1. Pos. o. D.
o. Dpf.
nimmt Dpf.
Hfe
Marie
Ei - a po - pei - a, mein sü - ßer Bu', Gibt mir kein
Hush - a - bye ba - by, my darl - ing son, No - bod - y
Bedeutend langsamer (Tempo II) (♩ = ca 72-80)
380
1. Vl. o. D.
(o. Dpf.) 1. 2. Solo tacet
Vla o. D.
(o. Dpf.) 1. 2. Solo tacet
1. Solo m. D. Vlc.
2. Solo m. D. Vlc.
2. Dpf. ab
3. Solo m. D. Vlc.
3. Dpf. ab
d. Übrig. o. D.
arco (o. Dpf.)
380 Bedeutend langsamer (Tempo II) (♩ = ca 72-80)

385
rit. - - Tempo I
Das neue ♩. entspricht dem letzten (rit.) ♩ des 3/4 Taktes
1. Fl.
1. Ob.
Englh.
Bkl. in B
Echo
1. Hr. in F o. D.
2.
gestopft
1. Trp. in F m. D.
(m. Dpf.)
1. Pos. m. D.
m. Dpf.
kl. Tr.
(deutlich)
Cel.
deutlich
Hfe
Marie
Mensch nix da - zu!
cares, ne'er a one.
Han - sel, spann' Dei - ne sechs Schim-mel an,
Jack - ie, go sad - dle your hors - es now,
Solo m. D.
1. Vl.
d. Übrig. o. D.
Vla
1. Solo (m. D.)
Vlc.
Dpf. ab
alle col legno geschl.
alle (o. Dpf.) col legno geschl.

390
1. Fl.
1. Ob.
Englh.
1. Kl. in B 2.
1. Fg.
1. Hr. in F o. D. 2.
1. Trp. in F m. D.
1. Pos. m. D.
kl. Tr.
Cel.
Hfe
gliss.
Marie
Gib sie zu fres-sen auf's neu — Kein Ha - ber fres-se sie,
Give them to eat and to spare, No oats to eat to-day,
390
col legno geschl.
o. Dpf.
arco
alle (o. Dpf.)
col legno geschl.
1. Vl. o. D.
2. Vl. o. D.
Vla o. D.
Vlc. o. D.
Kb.
390

395
molto rit.
Tempo II (aber etwas bewegter beginnen)
1. Fl.
1. Ob.
Englh.
1.
Kl. in B
2.
Bkl. in B
1. Fg.
Kfg.
offen
nimmt Dpf.
p Zeit lassen!
1.
Hr. in F o. D.
2.
Hr. in F o. D.
3.
offen (o. Dpf.)
nimmt Dpf.
Zeit lassen!
Hfe
Marie
Kein Was - ser sau - fe sie,
No wa - ter drink to day.
Lau - ter küh - le
Pur - est, cool - est
5 Soli m. D. 1. Vl.
m. Dpf. gew.
2. Vl.
Vla
Solo Vlc.
Kb.

rit.
400
ganz langsam
(quasi tempo I)
1. Fl.
1.
Kl. in B
2.
Bkl. in B
1. Fg.
Kfg.
mp
p dim.
ppp
pp
1. m.D.
Hr. in F
2. o.D.
(o. Dpf.)
m.Dpf.
nimmt Dpf.
gr. Tam-Tam
klingen lassen
Hfe
Marie
bemerkt, daß das Kind eingeschlafen ist
she notices that the child is asleep
Wein— muß — es sein! Lau - ter küh - le Wein— muß es sein!
wine— shall— it be, Pur - est, cool - est wine— shall it be.
5 Soli m.D. 1.Vl.
Dpf. ab
Vla
Solo Vlc.
mf
dim.
ppp dim.

405
1.
Kl. in B
2.
1. Fg.
1. Hr. in F
m.D.
1. Pos.
m.D.
(m. Dpf.)
pp
Hfe
405
Vla
Solo
Vlc.
d.Übrig.
1. Hälfte
ppp
2. Hälfte
405

410
415
Kfg.
Hr. in F m.D.
verlöschen
1. Pos. m.D.
Hfe
(Echo)
Marie
in Gedanken versunken
is now sunk in thought
1. Vl.
2. Vl.
Vla
Vlc.
Kb.
o.Dpf. get.
get.
pizz.

ELLIOTT CARTER

1908, New York—

Elliott Carter has become one of the important American composers of the second half of the century. After studying composition with Piston and Boulanger and receiving a degree from Harvard, Carter held positions as musical director of the Ballet Caravan and as a professor at St. John's College, Annapolis. Recently Carter has received various grants and awards and has become well known for his numerous well-wrought compositions as well as for his articulate comments and criticisms regarding contemporary music. Carter's early style has evolved into a complex non-serial approach which deals with large-scale temporal problems and with complicated melodic development. The excerpt here, from *Eight Etudes and a Fantasy for Woodwind Quartet,* is one of the first of Carter's works to deal with the problem of tempo proportions.

EIGHT ETUDES AND A FANTASY FOR WOODWIND QUARTET, 1950

This work grew out of a demonstration of the sound possibilities of woodwind instruments. The composition consists of eight etudes which concentrate on specific aspects of woodwind sound and technique (spacing, fluttertonguing, runs, etc.) and a fantasy which contrapuntally combines aspects of the etudes. It was first performed in 1952. One etude and part of the fantasy are reproduced here. All eight etudes should be heard before the fantasy is studied.

Etude No. 7 and an excerpt of the Fantasy

1. Study Etude No. 7 (a study on one note). Since pitch is a static parameter, what does Carter use to create motion and shape in this composition?
2. After listening to the eight etudes, study the Fantasy. What aspects does Carter use from the etudes?
3. Discuss the contrapuntal procedures used in the Fantasy. What characteristics does the opening melodic line have? How are the four voices brought into the texture? What techniques are used in the rest of the Fantasy?
4. Trace recurrences of the opening subject and the counter material.
5. Examine carefully the tempo changes in the Fantasy (*e.g.,* measures 13-19). How does Carter move from one tempo to another? What happens to the basic pulse? (Carter's process of change from one tempo to another has been referred to as "metric modulation." It would perhaps be more accurately described as "tempo modulation.") Diagram the whole Fantasy in terms of temporal aspects: tempo, rhythms, and linear density (amount of rhythmic activity in each line).

OTHER WORKS TO STUDY

Carter, Elliott: *Sonata for Cello and Piano* (1950)
String Quartet, No. 2 (1959)

ELLIOTT CARTER

Eight Etudes and a Fantasy for Woodwind Quartet

ETUDE NO. 7

20
f
p
f
p
ff
mf
p
ff
f
p
f
p
ff
f
p
f
p
f
p
ff
f
mf

25
ff
mf
mf
f
mf
ff sub.
mf
p
f sub.
mf
ff
p
f
ff
mf
mf
p
f sub.

30
mf
p
p
mf
p
p
p
p
pp
mf
p

FANTASY (Excerpt)

* In all changes of meter, the first note-value refers to the preceding meter, the second to the following. These changes should be carefully observed throughout.

cresc.
ff
mf
f
mf
f
p
25
Solo
mf
p
(p)
p
accomp.
Solo
mf
Solo
mf
cresc.
f
accomp.
p
cresc.
f
p
cresc.
f

30
mf
f marc.
(♩.. = 72)
f marc.
più f marc.
35
♩.. = ♩ = 72
ten.
ten.
espr.
dim.

40
espr.
p
f
mf
meno f
45
f marc.
cresc.
(♩ = 90)
ff

50
55
mf
f
p
mf marc.
marc.
menof
(p)

60
Fluttertongue
65
cresc.

p sub.
70
75
cresc.
cresc.

AARON COPLAND

1900, Brooklyn, New York—

Aaron Copland is one of many American composers whose early studies were with Nadia Boulanger in France during the 1920's. Copland has been active in promoting American music and has worked with the American Composer's Alliance and other societies to develop an interest in contemporary music in the United States. He has lectured and written about twentieth-century music for both professionals and laymen. Some of Copland's work is "abstract," *i.e.,* it has a concentrated style devoid of programmatic implications; other works, such as the one reproduced here, were written for a particular function.

APPALACHIAN SPRING, 1943-45 (excerpt)

Appalachian Spring is a ballet written for Martha Graham, commissioned by the Elizabeth Sprague Coolidge Foundation, and produced in 1944. Copland made a suite for orchestra from the ballet in 1945, at which time the work won a Pulitzer Prize. The ballet concerns a Pennsylvania pioneer celebration in spring, and centers around the marriage of a young couple and the building of their new home. The section here is from the first part of the ballet; both the elation and the religious feeling of the celebration are present in the music.

1. List the melodic motives used. What characteristics do they have?
2. Make a tonal diagram of the section. How do the tonalities relate to each other.? How is one tonal center set up and/or obscured?
3. Analyze the rhythmic structure of this section, particularly measures 53-85. How do accents support or conflict with the notated meter? Compare this work rhythmically with other works in the anthology.
4. Study the form of this section. What processes does Copland use to extend the opening material? What relationships exist between the large sections?

OTHER WORKS TO STUDY

Copland, Aaron: *Piano Variations* (1930)
Symphony, No. 3, II and III (1946)
Fantasy for Piano (1957)

AARON COPLAND

Appalachian Spring (excerpt)

5
10
I.
Fl.
II.
Ob.
I. II
I. Solo
a 2
(In A) I
Cl.
(In A) II
Solo
Fg.
I. II
I. Solo
a 2
Pfte.
Vl. I
Vl. II
Vla.
HALF
pizz.
Tutti
arco
Vc.
HALF
pizz.
Tutti
arco

7
marc.
a 2
15
Ob.
I. II
(In A) I
Cl.
(In A) II
f marc.
Cor. (F)
I. II
(cuivré)
Xylo.
Tabor
sf
8va
Pfte.
f marc.
Vl. I
Vl. II
Vla.
Vc.
pizz.
arco
p
f marc.

20
Solo
I.
Fl.
II.
Solo
mf
mf
Vl. I
pizz.
arco
pizz.
arco
20
2 Soli
div.
mf
Vl. II
arco
pizz.
arco
pizz.
div. (½ arco pizz.)
Vla.
pizz.
arco
pizz.
div. (½ arco pizz.)
Vc.
arco
pizz.
pizz.
arco
div. (½ arco pizz.)
mf
20
mf

8
non legato
25
I.
Fl.
II.
non legato
Ob.
I. II
non legato
(in A) I
Cl.
(in A) II
f non legato
f non legato
Cor. (F)
I. II
(Open) a 2
f marc.
Tr. (B♭)
I. II
(Open) a 2
f marc.
Trb.
I. II
a 2
f marc.
8va
Pfte.
f non legato (bell like)
2 Soli
Tutti
div.
f marc.
Vl. I
Vl. II
unis.
arco
f marc.
Vla.
unis.
arco
f marc.
Vc.
8va
f
f marc.

9
30
I.
Fl.
II.
Ob.
I. II
(in A) I
Cl.
(in A) II
Fg.
I. II
a 2
Cor. (F)
I. II
Tr. (B♭)
I. II
Trb.
I. II
Xylo.
8va
Pfte.
unis.
Vl. I
Vl. II
Vla.
unis.
arco
Vc.
f marc.
Tutti
Cb.
f marc.
ff

35
I.
Fl.
II.
a 2
Fg.
I. II
Cor. (F)
.. II
Tr. (B♭)
I. II
Trb.
I. II
Xylo.
8
8va
35
Pfte.
8va
35
Vl. I
Vl. II
Vla.
Vc.
Cb.
35

40
I.
Fl.
II.
Ob.
I. II
a 2
(in A) I
Cl.
(in A) II
Fg.
I. II
Cor. (F)
I. II
Tr. (Bb)
I. II
Trb.
I. II
Pfte.
8va
Vl. I
Vl. II
Vla.
Vc.
Cb.

10
45
I.
Fl.
II.
a 2
Ob.
I. II
(in A) I
Cl.
(in A) II
a 2
Fg.
I. II
I.
Cor. (F)
I. II
Tr. (B♭)
I. II
Trb.
I. II
10
45
8va
Vl. I
Vl. II
Vla.
Vc.
Cb.
10
45

Fl. I
Ob. I. II
(in A) I
Cl.
(in A) II
Fg. I. II
Cor. (F) I. II
Tr. (Bb) I. II
Trb. I. II
Timp.
Tri.
Pfte.
Vl. I
Vl. II
Vla.
Vc. Cb.
Solo
mf
50
Solo
p
I. Solo
p
Solo
p
Solo
p
Solo
p
I. Solo
p
11
Change to Bb
Change to Bb
a 2
sub. f marc.
a 2
sub. f marc.
f
p
50
f secco
50
11
f
pizz.
f
f
f
50
p
p
11
sub f marc.

55
I.
Fl.
II.
Ob.
I. II
(in B♭) I
Cl.
(in B♭) II
Fg.
I. II
a 2
Cor. (F)
I. II
Tr. (B♭)
I. II
Timp.
Xylo.
Pfte.
Vl. I
Vl. II
Vla.
Vc.
Cb.
marc.
arco
sf

60
Solo
Fl. I.
II.
Ob. I. II
(in B♭) I
Cl.
(in B♭) II
Cor. (F) I. II
a 2
Tr. (B♭) I. II
Timp.
Xylo.
60
ARPA
Pfte.
60
Vl. I
Vl. II
Vla.
Vc.
60

12
65
I.
Fl.
II.
non legato
non legato
Ob.
I. II
a 2
f
non legato
mf
(in Bb) I
Cl.
(in Bb) II
Cor. (F)
I. II
f marc.
Tr. (Bb)
I. II
f
mf
Arpa
p
Vl. I
f marc.
Vl. II
f marc.
Vla.
f marc.
Vc.
f marc.
Cb.
f marc.
mf
p
f
non legato
f marc.

70
I.
Fl.
II.
Ob.
I. II
a 2
(in B♭) I
Cl
(in B♭) II
Fg.
I. II
a 2
Cor. (F)
I. II
Tr. (B♭)
I. II
Trb.
I. II
I.
Tabor
70
Pfte.
70
Vl. I
Vl. II
Vla.
Vc.
Cb.
70

13 75
I.
Fl.
II.
Ob.
I. II
a 2
(in B♭) I
Cl.
(in B♭) II
Fg.
I. II
Cor. (F)
I. II
Tr. (B♭)
I. II
Trb.
I. II
Tabor
Pfte.
Vl. I
Vl. II
Vla.
Vc.
Cb.
f cresc.
cresc.
8va
fff
ff

80
85
Solo
I.
Fl.
II.
Ob.
I. II
a 2
(in B♭) I
Cl.
(in B♭) II
Fg.
I. II
Cor. (F)
I. II
marc.
Tr. (B♭)
I. II
Trb.
I. II
Timp.
Xylo.
Tabor
8va
Pfte.
Vl. I
Vl. II
Vla.
div.
p espress.
Vc.
Cb.
Vc.
Vc. e Cb.
sf
ff
ff-p
f
p espr.

14
Fl. I
90
Vl. I
Vl. II
Vla.
Vc.
Cb.
div.
unis.
p

I.
Fl.
II.
95
15
Solo
pp
Glock.
pp
Arpa
95
pp
Vl. I
95
15
Vl. II
Vla.
Vc.
Cb.
95
15
pp

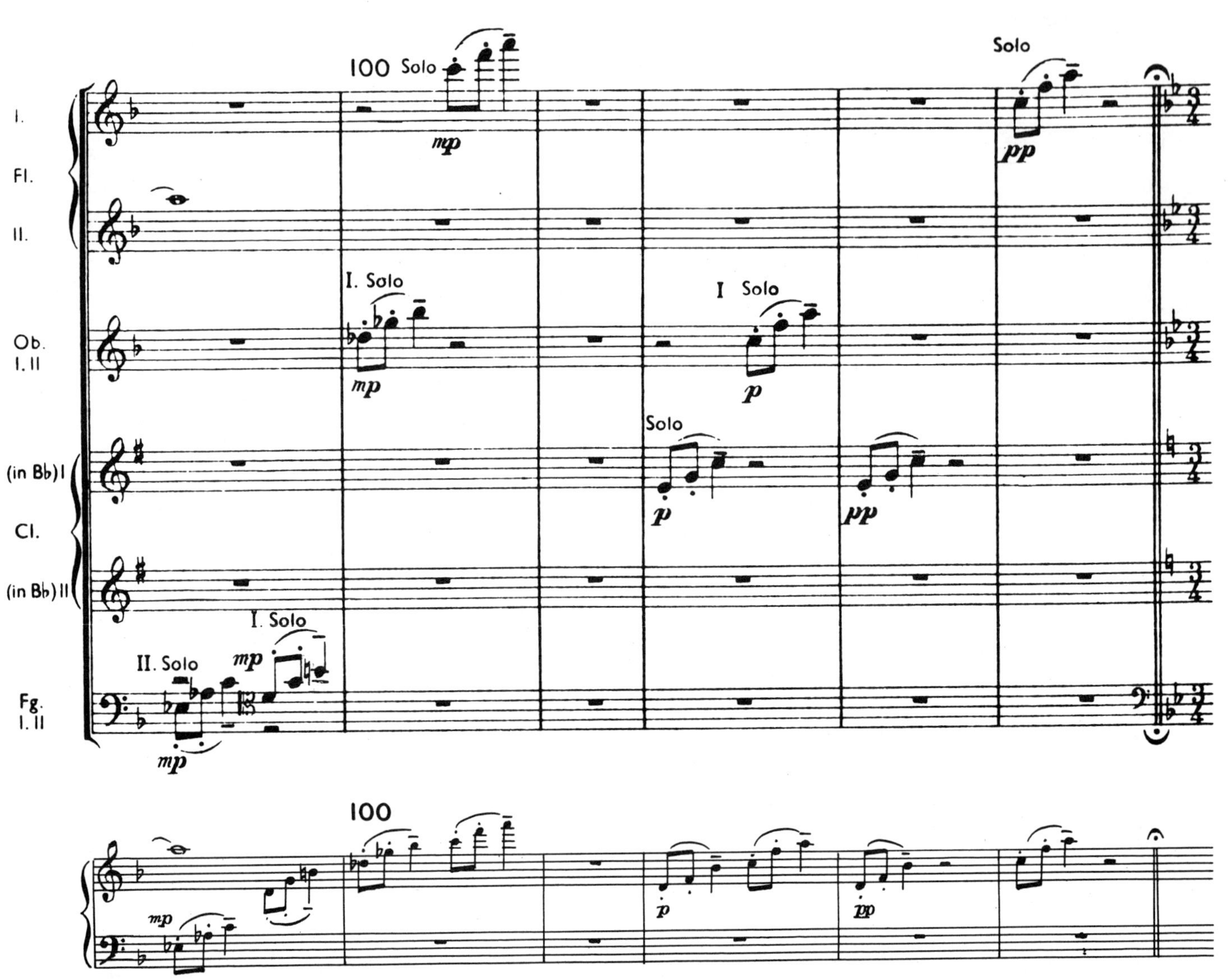
100
Solo
Solo
I.
Fl.
II.
I. Solo
I Solo
Ob.
I. II
Solo
(in B♭) I
Cl.
(in B♭) II
I. Solo
II. Solo
Fg.
I. II
mp
pp
p
100

KENNETH GABURO

1926, Raritan, New Jersey—

One of the important trends in composition in the 1950's and 1960's was a use of electronic sound sources, by themselves or in combination with other instruments. Kenneth Gaburo is an American composer whose works have become increasingly well known, a composer who has been chiefly concerned with electronic sound generation on the one hand and with the further exploration of live instrumental and vocal resources on the other. The two regions, when merged, result in a larger field of relations which Gaburo terms "compositional linguistics." Although linguistics in his case has a broad meaning (*e.g.,* music as language), it also suggests a multiplicity of specific meanings (one of which is the physio-acoustic domain of vocal transmission in the case of *Antiphony IV*).

Gaburo received degrees from the Eastman School of Music and the University of Illinois, and has studied in Rome and at the Princeton Seminar in Advanced Musical Studies. He has been the recipient of many grants, including a Guggenheim Fellowship, and is a skilled conductor as well as a composer. He has been professor of composition at the University of Illinois, and is presently Professor of Music at the University of California (San Diego).

Antiphony IV is composed for piccolo, bass trombone, double bass and two-channel tape. The right tape channel is composed of electronically generated sounds and is represented in the score by geometric designs which generalize phrase shape, duration, signal, and intensity characteristics. The left channel is composed of recorded vocal sounds and electro-mechanical transforms of these sounds, and is represented in the score by phonetic symbols. In live performance the instruments are amplified. The source of the phonemes (the phonetic symbols that represent classes of speech sounds) is the poem given below, written by Virginia Hommel, the composer's wife.

Antiphony IV is one in a series of "antiphonies" which explore the range of meaning of the word. In the largest sense Gaburo states that this work is not a paraphrase nor a literal representation of the poem, but presents a fluctuation ("antiphony") in thought between the poem and the composition as two separate entities.

ANTIPHONY IV, 1967

Poised above the sea as if to drop

Tense.

    heavy, hot

Waits

Gaining strength

And pours forth in soaring chill illusion!

    Virginia Hommel

1. Read the poem and listen to the composition without the score. Listen for the sounds used and any recurrence of sounds.
2. Read the introductory remarks and study the score. Notice how the various sounds have been notated.
3. The phonemes from the poem give a certain "predetermined" rhythm, structure, and color to the whole composition. Trace the phonemes and their transformations through the work.
4. Each one of the 21 sections of the piece presents a word of the poem. How are these sections different from each other? How are they the same? What relation does the poem have to the kinds of elements used in each section?

5. What parameters are important in creating shape (unity, variety, continuity) in this work? Diagram one of these parameters (dynamics, linear density, etc.) to see what shape emerges.

6. The composer has stated that this work should communicate an idea or expression. How do you think this communication takes place, if it does? What ideas or expressions are involved?

7. Listen to other compositions that use electronic sound sources and compare the sounds used to this work. Listen for important parameters and for shapes created in the compositions, or listen for "indeterminate" aspects. Try to find as many scores as possible to see the notation used. Suggested works are listed below, and various collections are available.

OTHER WORKS TO STUDY

Arel, Bülent: *Stereo Electronic Music No. 1* (1964)
Babbitt, Milton: *Composition for Synthesizer* (1964)
Badings, Henk: *Evolutions* (1958)
Berio, Luciano: *Differences* (1958-1960)
Cage, John: *Aria with Fontana Mix* (1958)
Variations IV (1965)
Gaburo, Kenneth: *Lemon Drops* (1965)
For Harry (1966)
Stockhausen, Karlheinz: *Gesang der Jünglinge* (1955-1956)
Kontakte (1959-1960)
Stüdie II (1954, first electronic score to be published, 1956)
Ussachevsky, Vladimir: *Piece for Tape Recorder* (1955)
Varèse, Edgar: *Poème électronique* (1958)
Déserts (1954)

NOTES

piccolo, bass trombone, double bass, voice (left channel speaker system), electronic sound (right channel speaker system), 1966-1967

General Remarks

Piccolo sounds 8va higher than written. Double bass 8va lower except for harmonics which sound where written.

Double bass part is written for a 5 string instrument. Should one not be available, the *lower* notes which fall out of range of the conventional 4 string instrument may be transposed up an octave, *e.g.*

Left channel tape notation: (a) conventional note heads=normal voice, (b) ẋ =filtering operations on textual phonemes, (c) ⌞ =f.m., a.m. operations, and electronic transforms of "central" frequency noted.

Right channel tape notation:
(a) geometric designs such as

 =

noise bands.

(b)  =

high frequency square wave clusters.

(c)  =

low modulated pulse trains.

(d)  =

clangorous signals.

(e)  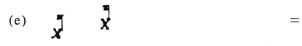 =

percussive, synthesized "bass" modulated signals.

Additionally, these signals are generalized into an amplitude contour display, *e.g.*, sections 1-9 are all:

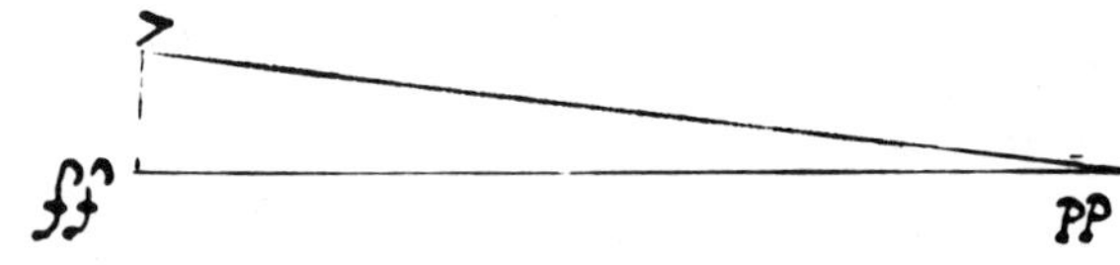

Structurally, the instruments parallel these contours. Therefore a basis for articulating large phrase gestures obtains.

Accidentals apply only to those notes with which they are associated.

Antiphony IV should be performed without a conductor. The signals on the left channel are accurately notated with regard to attacks, etc., and provide a sufficient reference point for the performers.

The tape which accompanies the score is noncontinuous. That is, it is arranged in terms of an elaborate cuing set-up, and will require another performer to operate it. It is necesary that the sound immediately following the leader strip for an up-coming cue be placed in contact with the pb head. With high quality equipment optimum tape travel should be available instantly.

Double bass and piccolo are amplified (see arrangement below). Their speaker outlets should be placed high and away from the performing area (*e.g.,* in front of the proscenium on a conventional stage).

Total signal balance, *i.e.,* l-r channels, amplified instruments will have obtained when (a) each transmits corresponding intensity, (b) no masking takes place between or among the sources, (c) the total output effect is vibrant, burning, and piercing.

Other Symbols used in the Score:

P = piccolo
T = trombone
B = double bass
R = right channel (right speaker)
L = left channel (left speaker)
f.t. = double bass finger tremolo (*i.e.,* alternate fingers as fast as possible)
b.p. = double bass bow-pizz. (side of bow)
n.v. = normal vibrato
m.v. = molto vibrato
s.v. = senza vibrato
s.p. = sul ponticello (bass)

N = normale, *i.e.,* return to normal playing after some special effect, also normal (notated) pitch, *c.f.,* below.

o = bass harmonics
o = trombone senza vibrato, however approaching the quality of harmonics.
o = piccolo:
(a) harmonics when possible
(b) very senza vibrato where (a) is not possible
(c) whistle tones in soft dynamics and high registers.

Grace notes into notes or rests are to be as short durationally as possible.

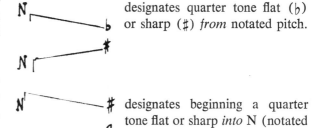

N —— ♭ / N —— ♯ designates quarter tone flat (♭) or sharp (♯) *from* notated pitch.

N —— ♯ / N —— ♮ designates beginning a quarter tone flat or sharp *into* N (notated pitch).

Articulation Marks:

▬ = full notated value. If used with successive notes legato is implied.
staccato = as short a duration as possible.

= slightly less than full value. In successive notes the effect is equal to minimal duration "breath" marks.
> = accent, and may accompany any of the above.

Slashes across stems always mean flutter-tongue (piccolo, trombone), tremolo (double bass), and notes associated should be played as fast as possible.

Slashes between notes,  signify tremolos to be played as fast as possible.

ARRANGEMENT

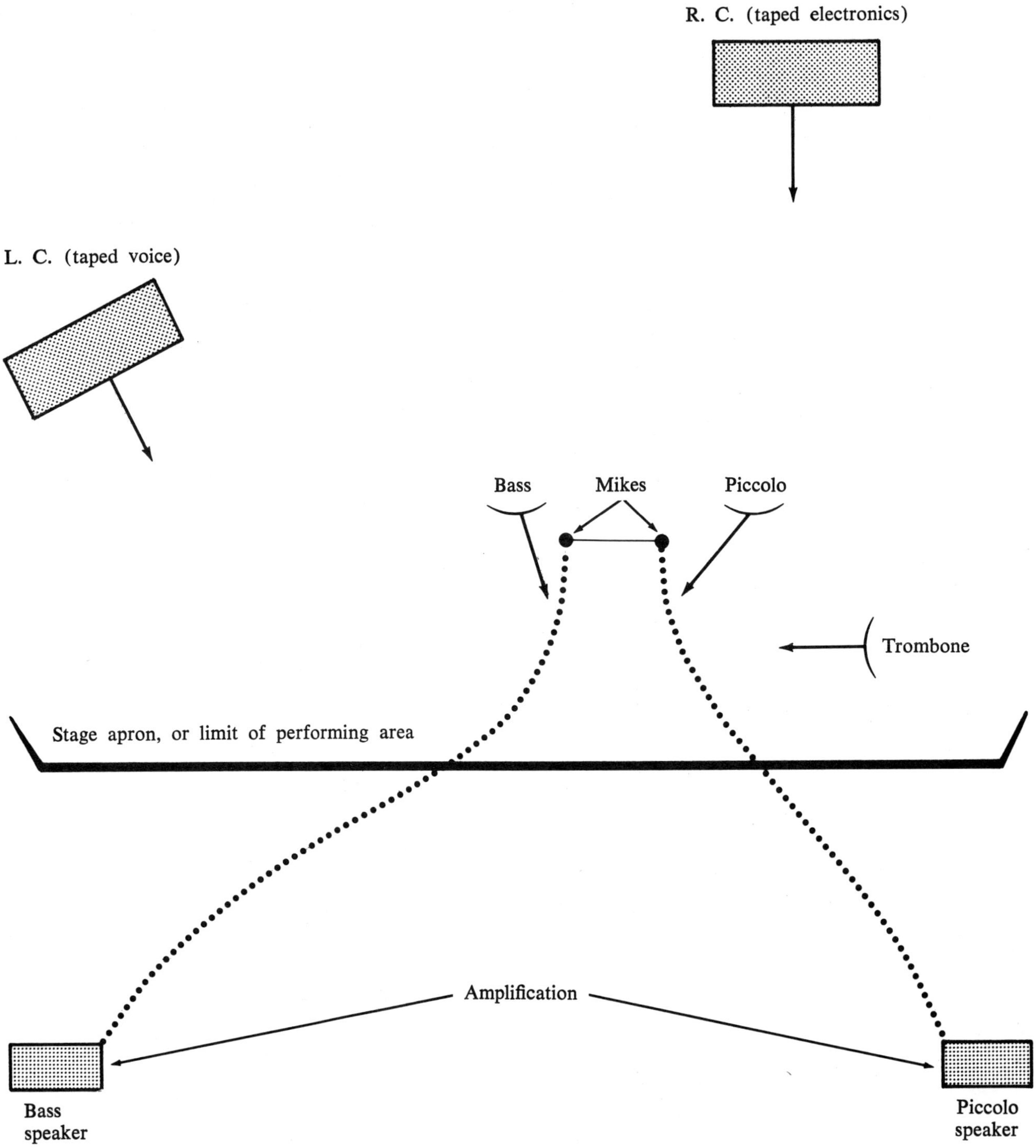

R. C. (taped electronics)

L. C. (taped voice)

Bass

Mikes

Piccolo

Trombone

Stage apron, or limit of performing area

Amplification

Bass speaker

Piccolo speaker

KENNETH GABURO

Antiphony IV

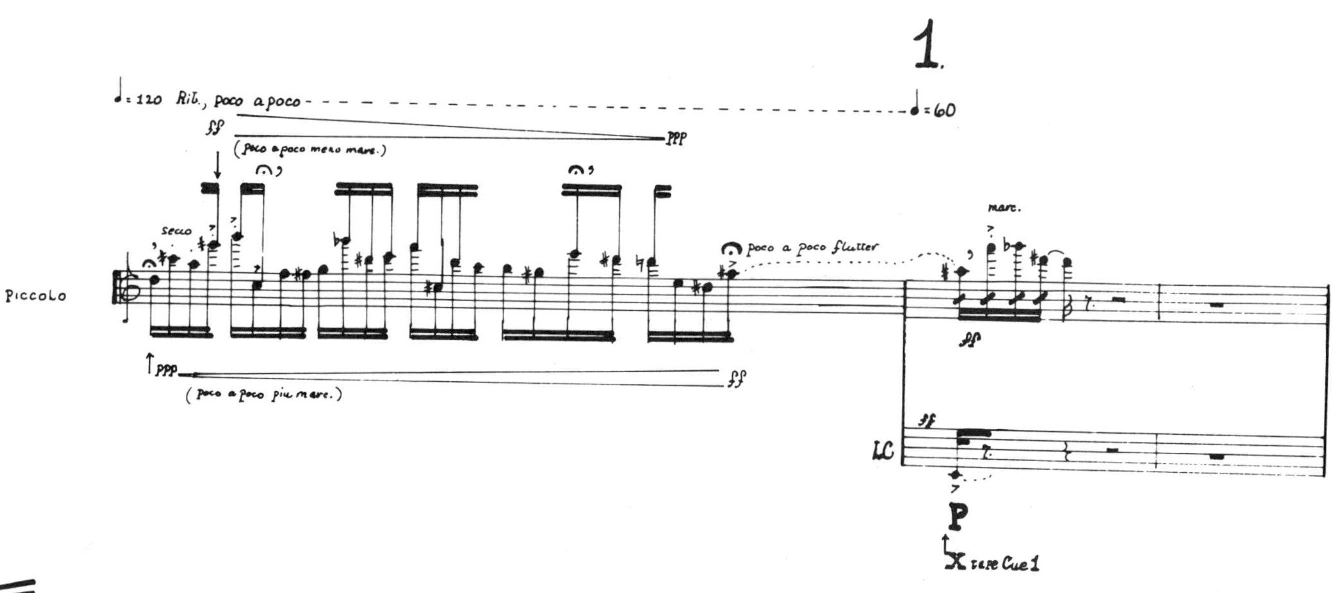

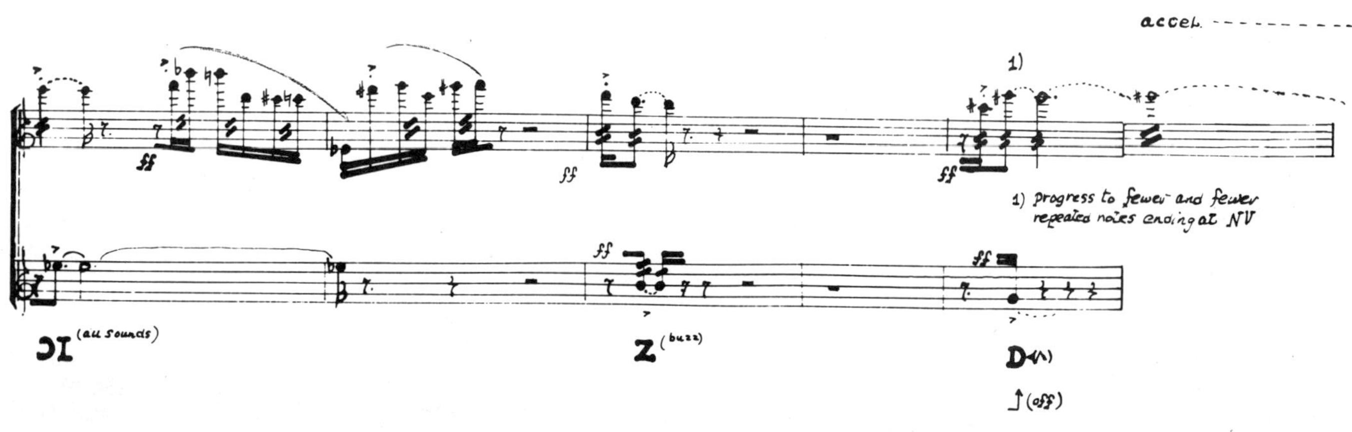

2.

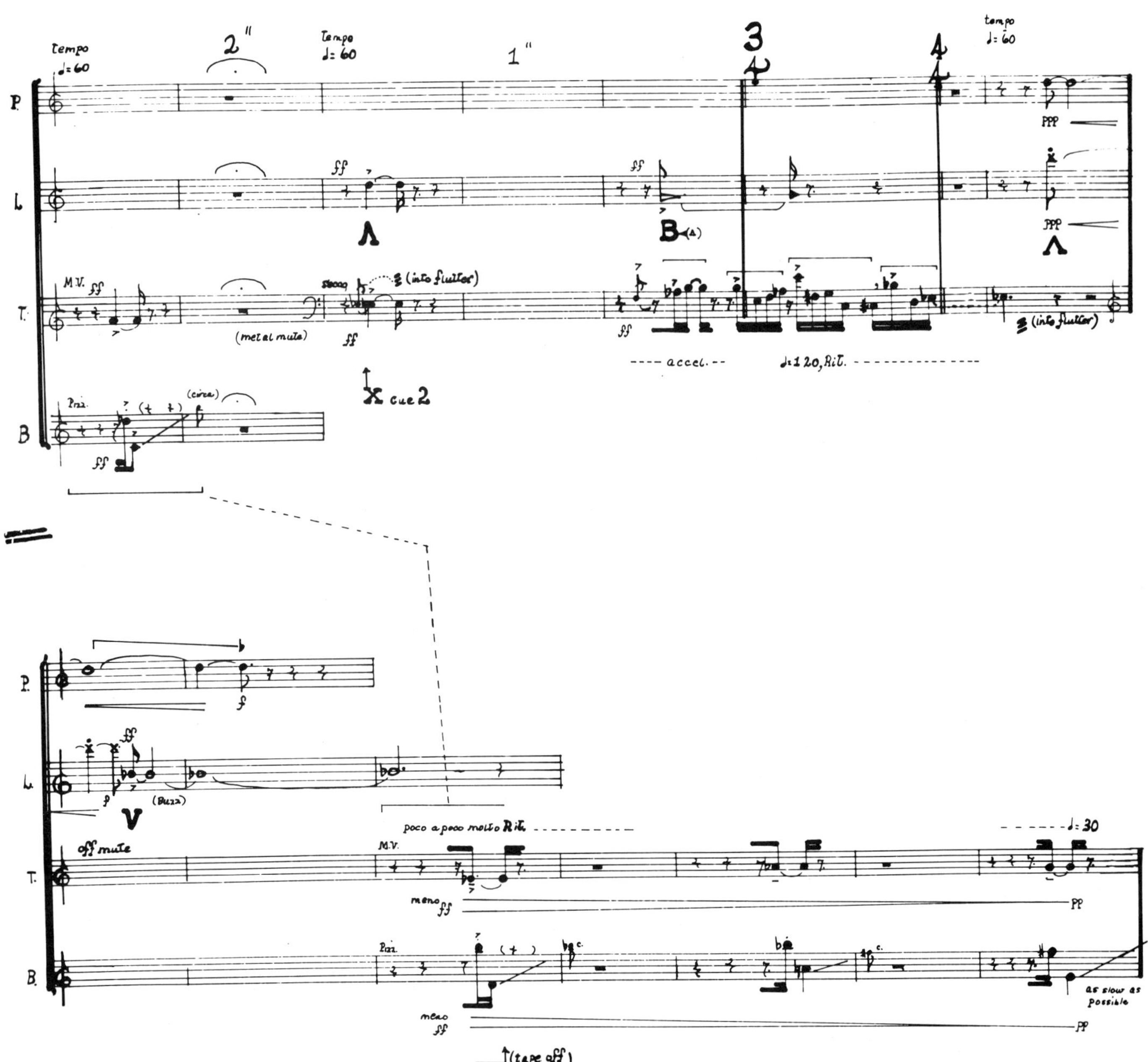

tempo
♩= 60
2"
1"
3
4
P.
L.
T.
B.
M.V.
(metal mute)
(into flutter)
cue 2
accel.
♩= 120, Rit.
(circa)
Pizz.
(Buzz)
off mute
poco a poco molto Rit.
♩= 30
meno ff
as slow as possible
(tape off)

10"
3.
d.bass gliss.
cue 3
(anticipate decay of d. bass gliss.)
♩=120
4.
P.
S (gliss)
(tape off)
T.
1) don't release until (L) f# enters
Poco a Poco Rit.
♩=60
Rit.
T.
arco
B.
pizz.
cue 4

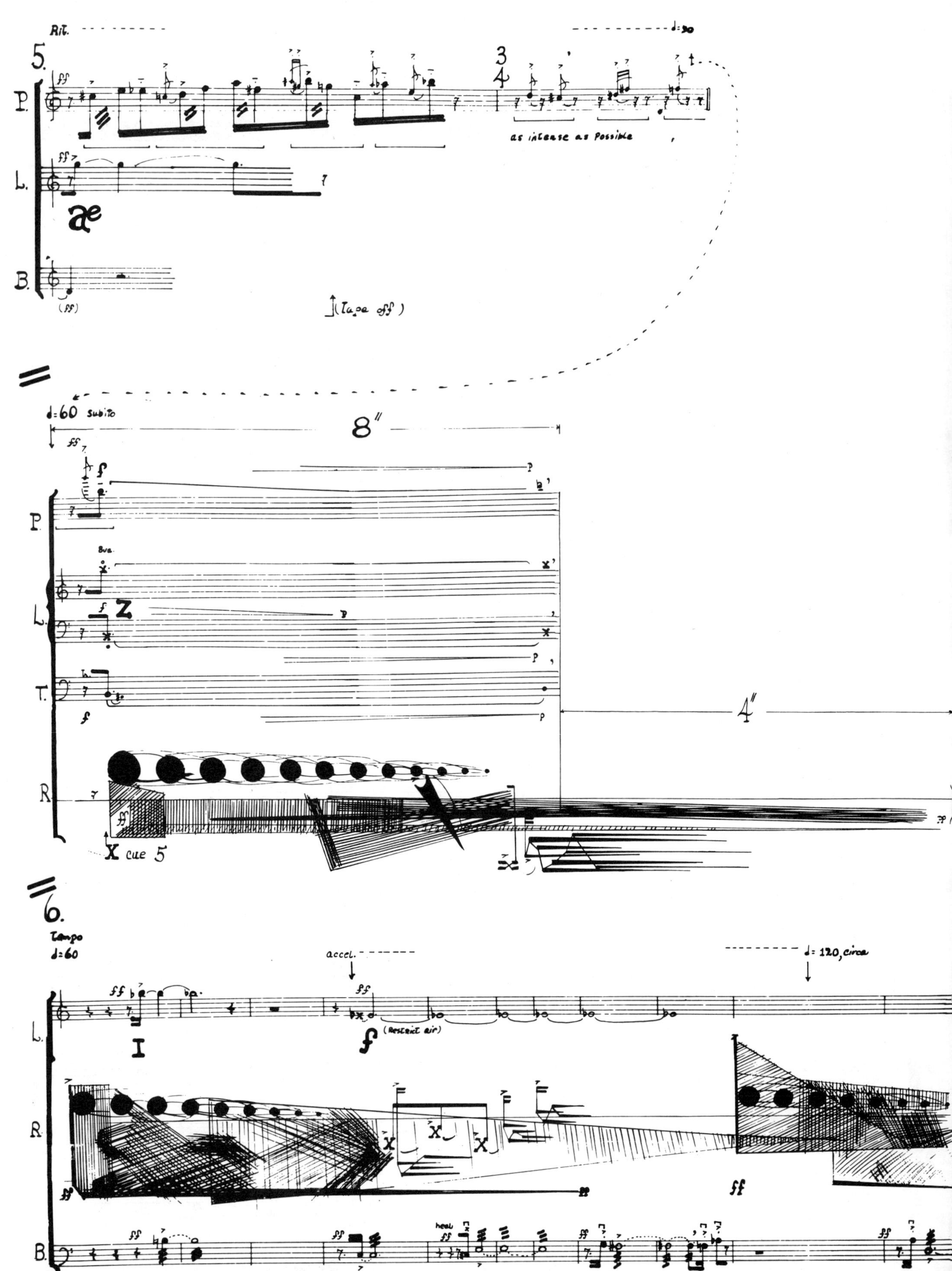
Rit.
5.
P.
L.
B.
as intense as possible
(Tape off)
♩=60 subito
8″
8va
T.
R.
4″
X cue 5
6.
Tempo
♩=60
accel.
(Restrict air)
♩=120, circa

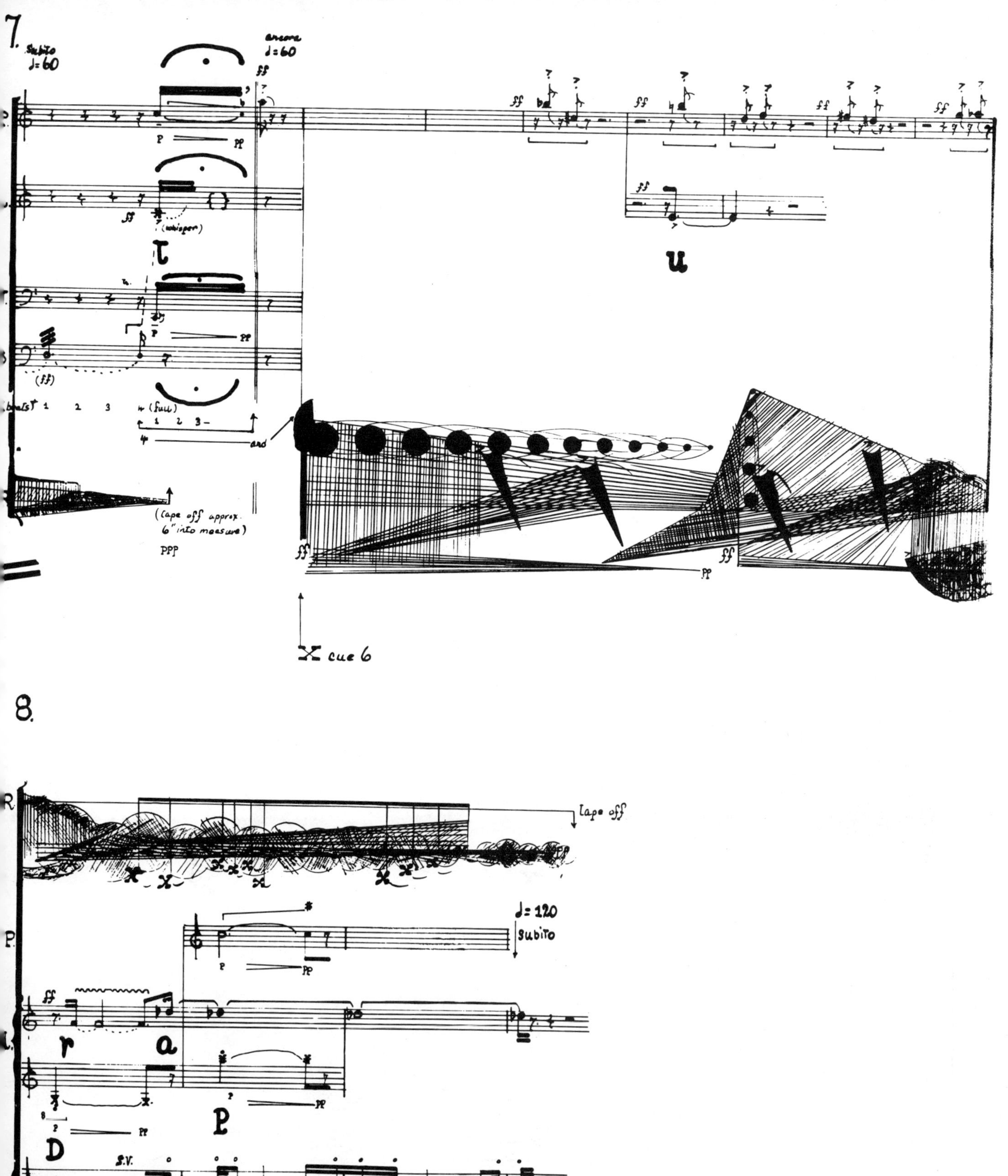
7.
Subito ♩=60
ancora ♩=60
(whisper)
T
u
beats 1 2 3 4 (full)
1 2 3
4 and
(tape off approx. 6" into measure)
ppp
cue 6
8.
tape off
♩=120
subito
r
a
P
D
S.V.
N.V.
Pizz.
arco s.p.

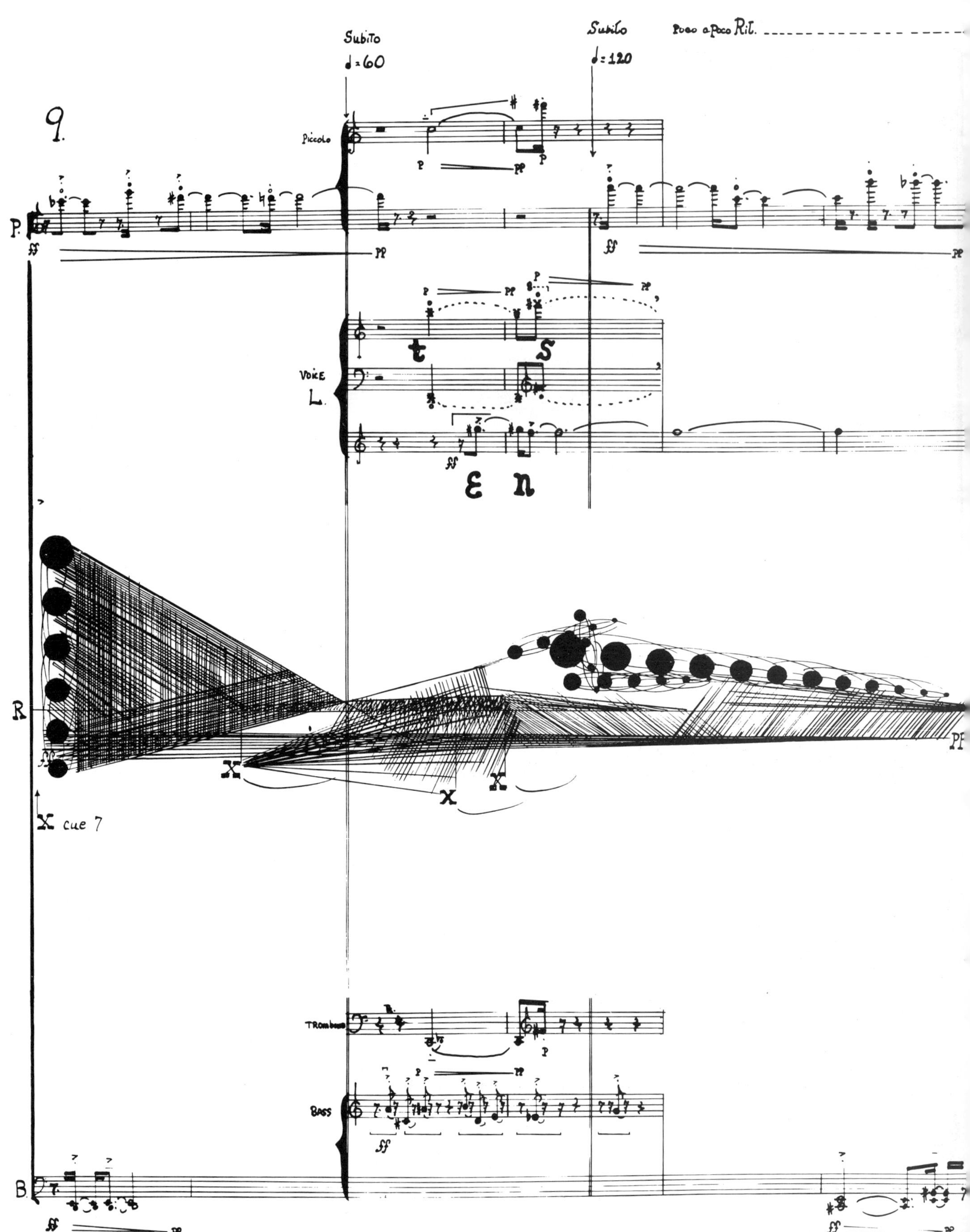
9.
Subito
♩=60
Subito
♩=120
Poco a Poco Rit.
Piccolo
P.
Voice
L.
R
X cue 7
Trombone
Bass
B

♩=60
Rit.
11.
♩=40
♩=60
Rit.
♩=30
1) N.V.
(breathy)
gliss
quasi dolce
(libero)
1) fermatas in this passage = about 4 ♩'s at 60 MM
(tape off)
P.
L.
♩=60
T.
B.
R.
♩=60
7''
(silence)
(Pizz.)
X cue B

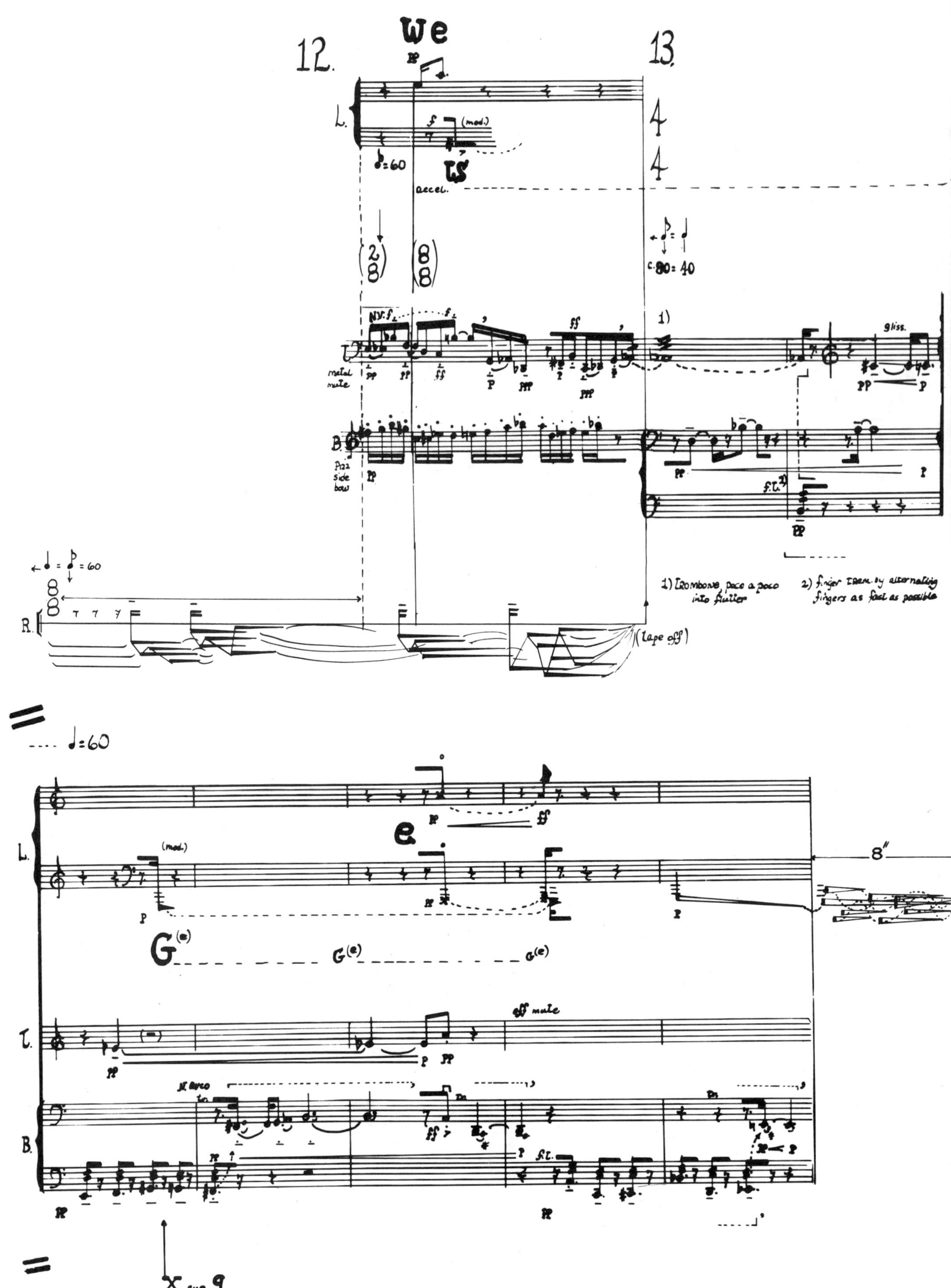

12.
We
13.
L.
(mod.)
accel.
c.80 = 40
metal mute
gliss.
B.
Pizz side bow
1) Trombone poco a poco into flutter
2) finger TREM. by alternating fingers as fast as possible
R.
(tape off)
e
G(e)
8″
off mute
T.
N. Arco
X cue 9

ancora
♩=60
14.
3
P
L.
T.
B.
R.
M.V.
S.V.
S.P.
pp
ff
p
pp — mp — pp

4/4

15. Subito

♩=120

P.

pp ff pp

(very breathy)

pp

(very breathy)

Subito

♩=120, rit. - - - - - ♩=40

L.

pp

a

T.

f

2)

(mute on)

pp

2) trombone cuts off on tape entrance

Molto Liberamente

(side of bow pizz. slow to fast as possible to slow

S.P.

B.

pp

f marc.

ff

B.P.

R.

(tape off)

ppp

X cue 10

P.

pp ff pp

ff

pp ff pp

pp ff

L.

n

pp

ff

D

pp ff

T.

pp

off mute

(breathy)

pp

N.

ff

pp < ff

R.

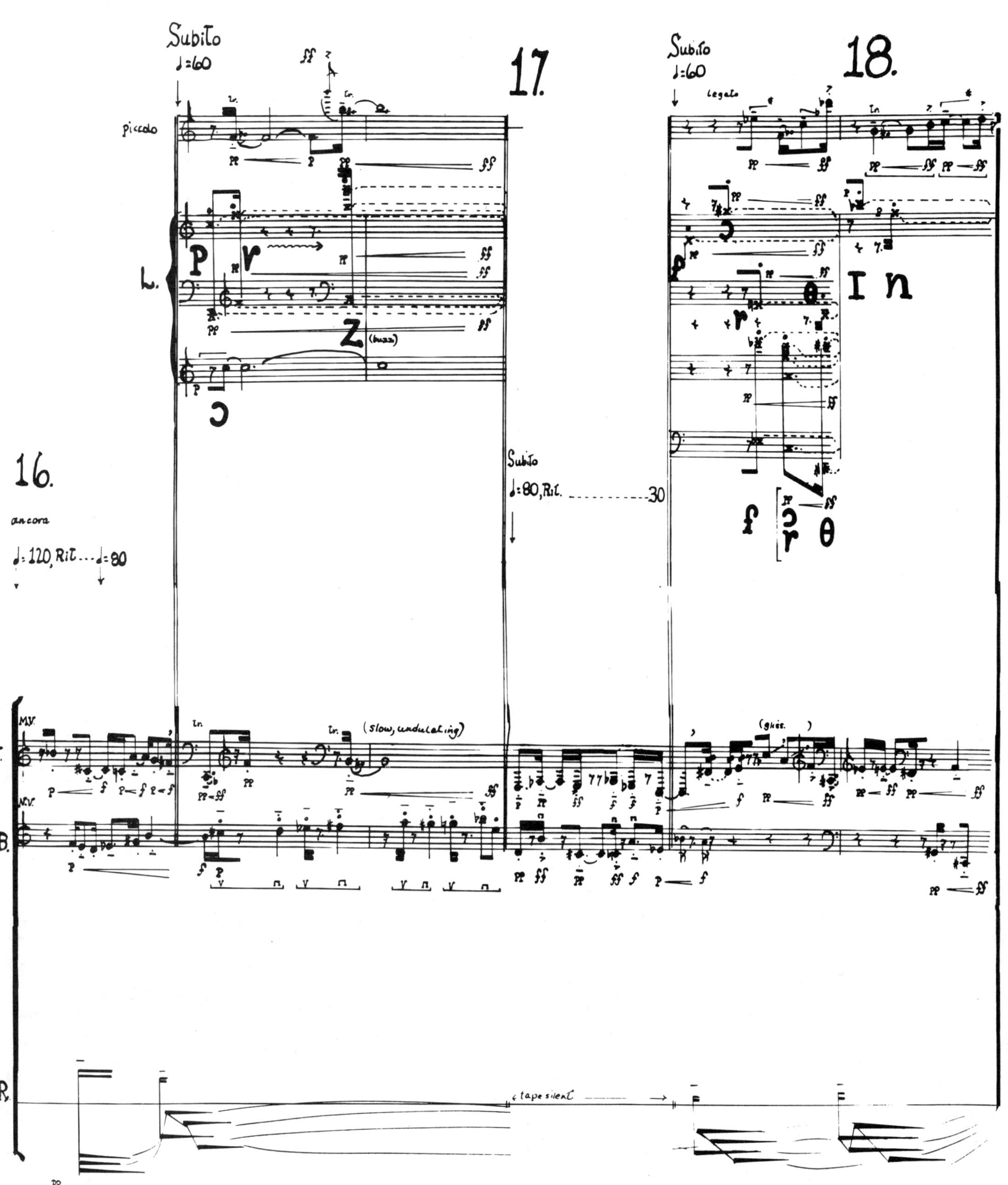

Subito
♩=60
17.
Subito
♩=60
18.
Legato
piccolo
L.
(buzz)
16.
ancora
♩=120, Rit. . . ♩=80
Subito
♩=80, Rit. ----------30
M.V.
T.
N.V.
B.
(slow, undulating)
(gliss.)
R.
tape silent

19.

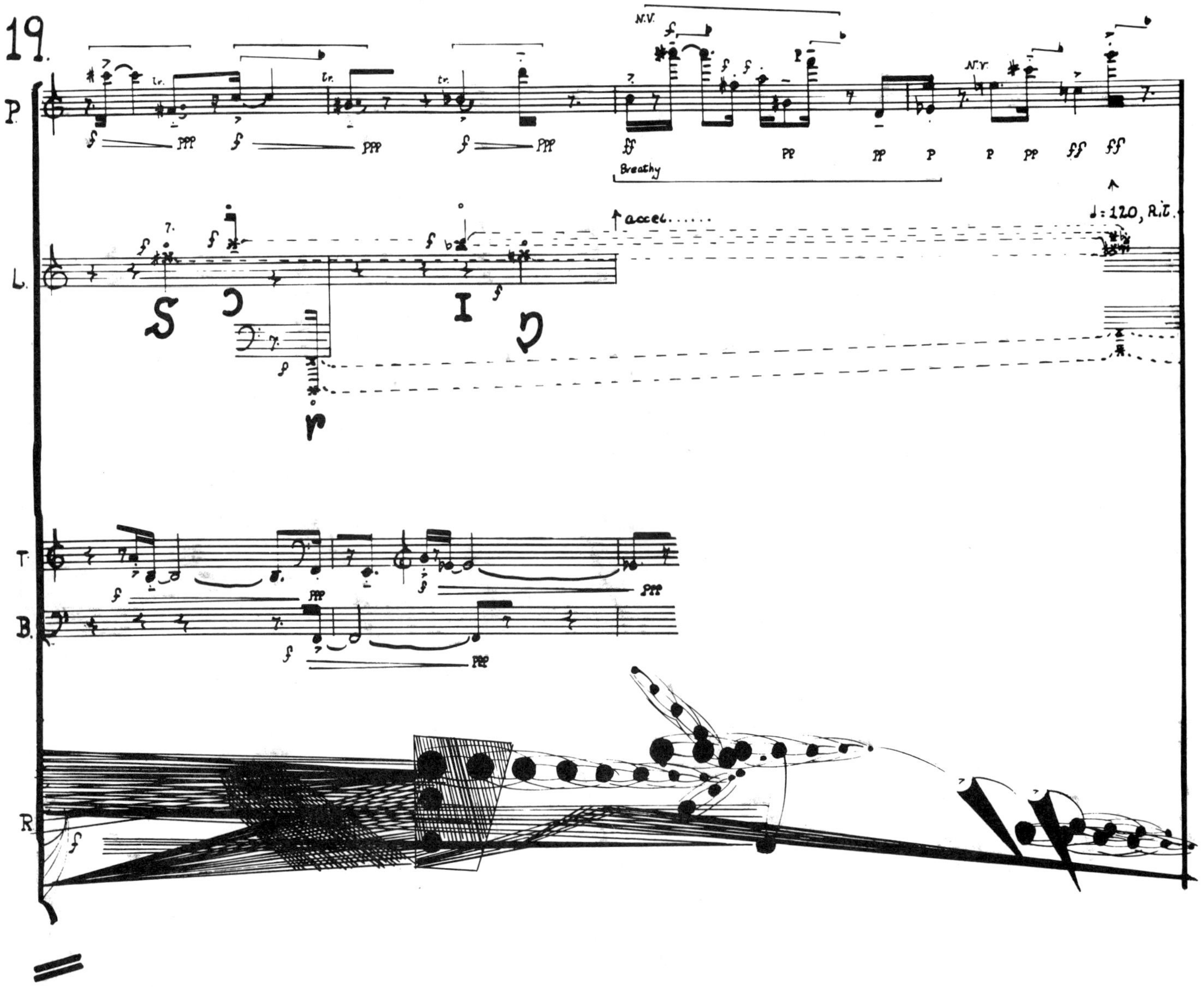

P

N.V.

tr.

f ppp f ppp f ppp

ff pp pp p p pp ff ff

Breathy

L.

accel......

♩=120, R.T.

T.

B.

f ppp

R.

f

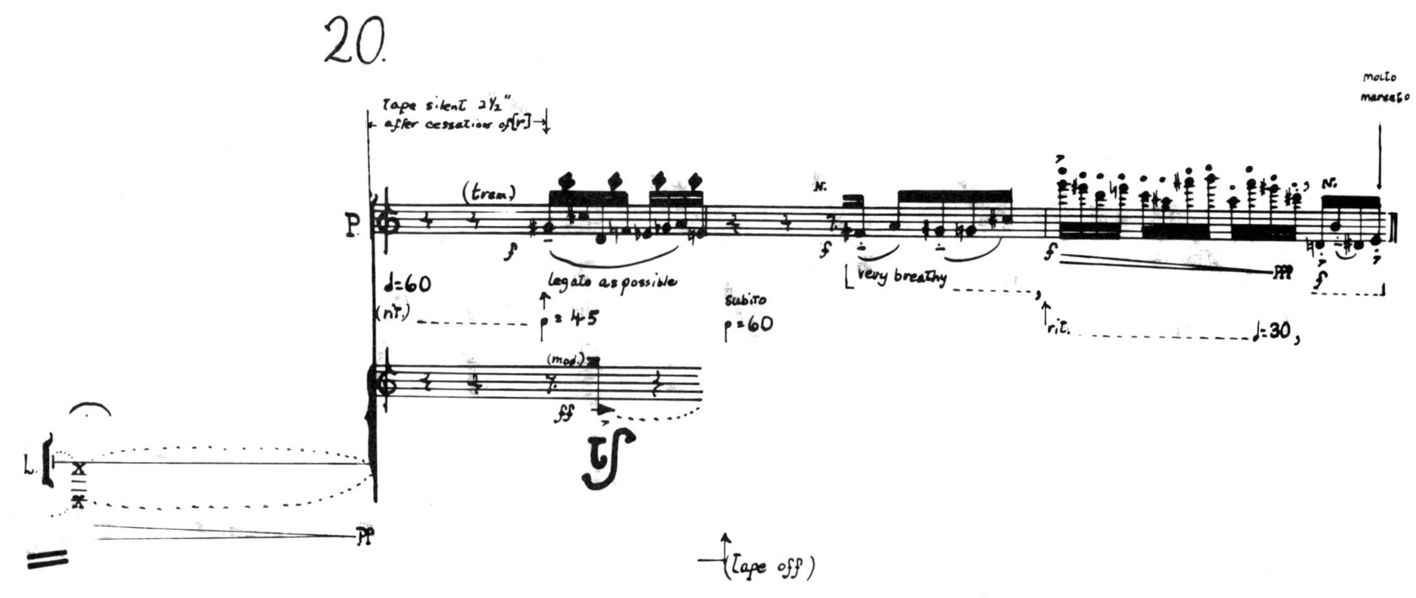

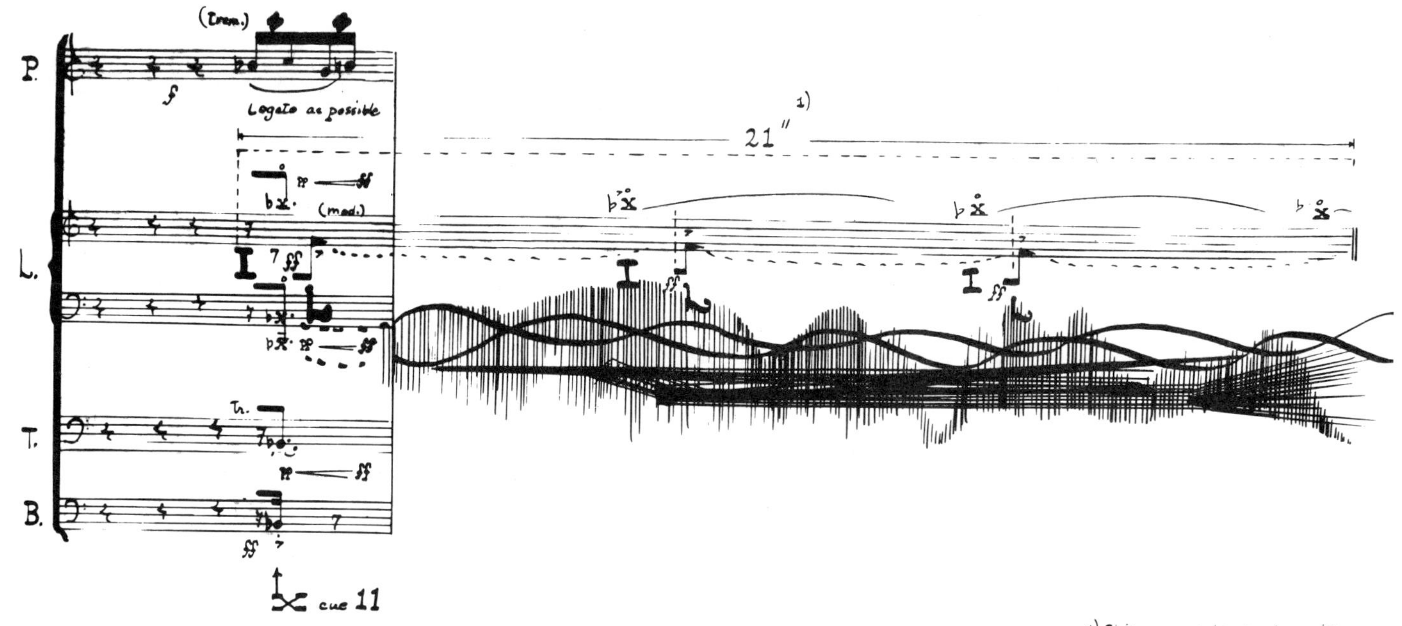

1) This passage breaks down into 3 sequences of 7" each, prior to # 21.

21.

3/4 Subito ♩= 90

4/4

P.

L.

T.

B.

12/25/67

PAUL HINDEMITH

1895, Hanau, Germany—1963, Frankfort, Germany

Paul Hindemith was a German composer who was active in the musical life of his country and of Europe as a composer, writer, teacher, and performer of many instruments, primarily the viola. After 1929 he spent much time outside of Germany, organizing the musical life of Turkey and coming to the United States in the late 1930's. He served as head of the music department at Yale and returned to Germany near the end of his life. He is well known as a prolific composer, having written works for almost every instrument, as a teacher of many other composers, and as one of the prominent speculative theorists of the twentieth century. His ideas presented in the volumes of the *Craft of Musical Composition* have acted as the point of departure for compositional and analytical approaches.

Hindemith's music has been labeled as neoclassic, and there are often elements that are reminiscent of an earlier era. Hindemith's main concern in most of his music is with discipline and craftsmanship. In his writings and his music Hindemith expresses his fondness for traditional concepts of organization and design combined with newer materials.

STRING QUARTET, Op. 22, 1922

This quartet is the third of six string quartets writen by Hindemith. It is in five movements; the movement reproduced here is the second and follows an opening "Fugato" movement. The quartet combines classic structures with twentieth-century rhythms and sonorities and with Hindemith's own clear sense of proportion.

Second Movement, Schnelle Achtel; Sehr energisch (excerpt)

1. Listen to the whole movement. What creates form in this movement? List the elements that contribute to sectionalization. What relationships do the sections have to one another?
2. Analyze the rhythmic organization of the movement. What metric and rhythmic patterns are used? How are phrases and larger sections organized rhythmically? Compare this movement with the rhythmic organization of Stravinsky's "Triumphal March of the Devil" from *L'Histoire du Soldat.*
3. Study the harmonic and tonal material of this movement and compare it to the material of the fugue from *Ludus Tonalis.*
4. Analyze the melodic structure of this movement. Consider rhythmic and pitch patterns used, treatment of material, structural pitches, etc. for each important line.
5. Listen to the whole quartet and compare it to others in this anthology.

PAUL HINDEMITH

String Quartet, Op. 22

SECOND MOVEMENT (Excerpt)

10
F
sul G
sul G
15

20
mf
mf
mp
mp
cresc.
cresc.
cresc.
cresc.
25
f
f
f
f
ff dim.
ff dim.
ff dim.
ff dim.

G
30
mf
cresc.
mf
cresc.
mf
cresc.
cresc.
mf
35
Poco ritenuto
ff
molto dim.
p
ff
molto dim.
pp
ff
molto dim.
pp
molto dim.
ff
pp
H
a tempo (grazioso)
8
40
pp sehr zart
3
3
sul D
ppp
ppp
pp

45
50
(5/8)
(5/8)
55
ppp
cresc.
mf
mp
pp
p

I
pp
pizz.
pp
p
mp
60
poco cresc.
poco cresc.
p cresc.
65
p
p
mf
K
mf
mf
arco
mp
pizz.
mf

70
75
arco
dim.
mf
80
Poco ritenuto
p

L
85
Ruhig (ein wenig langsamer als vorher)
pp
pp
pp
pp
(pp)
(pp)
90
dim.
dim.
simile
dim.
ppp
ppp
pp
pp
pp
ppp
95
Immer im gleichen ruhigen Zeitmaß
(etwas trocken)
M
cresc.
p
cresc.

Hindemith, LUDUS TONALIS, 1942

Ludus Tonalis ("Game of Tones") is a contemporary *Well-Tempered Clavier.* It contains a Prelude and a Postlude (which is a retrograde inversion of the Prelude), 12 fugues, and 11 interludes. The "key" arrangement is based on Hindemith's theory of tone relationships (see the *Craft of Musical Composition,* Vol. I). The order of the fugues:

C G F A E E♭ A♭ D B♭ D♭ B F♯

reflects Hindemith's ordering of the twelve tones as related to C (G is the closest, F♯ the most distant, relationship).

The interlude reproduced here follows the Fugue in F and precedes the Fugue in A, also reproduced here. The position of the interlude is reflected in its tonal plan.

Interlude and Fugue in A

1. Analyze the interlude for form. What creates sectionalizing points?
2. Analyze the cadences for sonorities used and approaches to these sonorities. What generalizations can be made? Compare the cadences with the cadences in the fugue.
3. Compare the melodic, rhythmic, and harmonic material in the interlude to other piano compositions in the anthology. What differences are there in Hindemith's use of piano timbre as compared to Schoenberg's and Bartók's?
4. Write out the basic material of the fugue.
5. Study the fugue for whatever contrapuntal techniques and devices are used (inversion, stretto, developmental episode, etc.).
6. What significance do the three sections of the fugue have?
7. What kind of tonal plan is used in the fugue? Why is "Fugue in A" used as a title?
8. What other elements are important in this fugue besides pitch material?
9. Compare this fugue subject to subjects in Bach's *Well-Tempered Clavier.* Compare the fugue to Bach's fugues, to the opening of Carter's *Woodwind Fantasy,* and to Stravinsky's *Dylan Thomas* Prelude for material and contrapuntal techniques. Also study other fugues in *Ludus Tonalis.*

OTHER WORKS TO STUDY

Hindemith, Paul: *Kleine Kammermusik,* Op. 24, No. 2 (1922).
Mathis der Maler (1934)
Six Chansons (1939)
Four Temperaments (1940)
Twelve Madrigals (1958)
Mass (1963)

PAUL HINDEMITH

Ludus Tonalis

INTERLUDE

25
p
mf
30
p
35
mp
p
40
pp
FUGUE IN A
With energy (𝅗𝅥 108)
Fuga quarta in A
f

5
p
10
mf
p
15
f
20
25
f
allargando
ff

Slow, grazioso (♩ ca. 63)
pp
30
mp
35
pp
p
40
mf
8
pp
mp
pp

45
Tempo primo
f
50
55
mf
f
60

65
70
ff
allargando
75

CHARLES IVES

1874, Danbury, Connecticut—1954, New York

An American composer and prominent insurance man, Charles Ives was active in musical composition in the first quarter of the twentieth century. Although he lived until 1954, he heard few of his works performed, and only since his death has his music become well known. Ives experimented with many ideas novel in the early twentieth century, such as polytonality, non-tertian harmony, and cluster-chords. Many of Ives's works reflect his American environment by their reference to hymns, dance tunes, and popular songs. These tunes provide germ motives, which are developed and varied in a complicated and frequently heterogeneous texture.

SECOND SONATA FOR VIOLIN AND PIANO, 1906-1910

The movement that follows is the third and last of the *Second Violin Sonata.* Subtitled "The Revival," the movement is suffused with the hymn tune quoted on the following page.

Third Movement, The Revival

1. Trace the use of the "cantus firmus" hymn tune in this movement. How does Ives treat his material? Compare this treatment with other compositions based on preexistent material, *e.g.,* Josquin des Prés, *Pange Lingua Mass* and J. S. Bach, *Cantata,* No. 4.
2. Analyze the harmonic and tonal material. How does it compare with the "standard" harmonization of the hymn tune? What kinds of harmonic structures are used? What tonal centers are established? Compare the pitch material to other compositions of the same time, *e.g.,* Debussy, *Preludes;* Berg, *Songs,* Op. 2; and Webern, *Six Pieces,* Op. 6.
3. Study the rhythmic characteristics of this movement (metric structure, cross rhythms, etc.). Compare Ives's treatment of rhythm with the Bartók *Mikrokosmos,* No. 148.
4. Describe the melodic structure of this work. What ideas are used and how are they treated?

OTHER WORKS TO STUDY

The first two movements of this sonata
Ives, Charles: *The Unanswered Question* (1908)
Concord Sonata for Piano (1909-1915)
Symphony, No. 4, II (1910-1916)

COME, THOU FOUNT OF EV'RY BLESSING

Robert Robinson

John Wyeth

Come, Thou fount of ev'-ry bless-ing, Tune my heart to sing Thy
grace; Streams of mer-cy, nev-er ceas-ing, Call for songs of loud-est
praise. Teach me some me-lo-dious son-net, Sung by flam-ing tongues a-
bove; Praise the mount, I'm fixed up-on it! Mount of Thy re-deem-ing love.

CHARLES IVES

Second Sonata for Violin and Piano

THIRD MOVEMENT, THE REVIVAL

C
rit. freely
arco
più mosso
ten.
(Ped.)
poco ten.
pizz.
arco
very slowly again
rit.
Ped
faster (allegretto con moto)
poco rit.
a tempo
poco rit.
D Allegretto
senza sordino

E
f
allegro con moto
10
f
3
l.h.

F
ff
G
allegro assai (con fuoco)
H

ff
1
fff
fff
dim. e rit.
Repeat 2 or 3 times
decr. & rit. gradually to p very slowly
pp
ppp
dim. e rit.
pp
ppp

VINCENT PERSICHETTI

1915, Philadelphia—

Vincent Persichetti is a well-known American composer and teacher. He is a pianist, organist, and conductor and studied at Combs College and the Curtis Institute of Music. He has been head of the composition departments of Combs College and the Philadelphia Conservatory, and since 1948 has been a member of the faculty of the Juilliard School of Music.

Persichetti's works include symphonies and other works for orchestra, several pieces for band, string quartets, vocal works, and a series of serenades, including one for solo tuba. His compositions are tightly-knit and often contrapuntal, and although the basic structures are tonal, there are sometimes bi-tonal "layers."

Persichetti is active as a teacher, composer, lecturer, and writer and has contributed several books and articles about contemporary music and its structure.

DIVERTIMENTO FOR BAND, 1950

This suite of six movements was premiered in 1950 by the Goldman Band. The "March" reproduced here is the last movement of the *Divertimento* and presents a spirited finale to the contrasting moods of the previous movements.

Sixth Movement, March

1. Study the instrumentation and compare the use of the instruments to the orchestral works in the anthology, such as Schuller's "Little Blue Devil."
2. What kinds of harmonic structures are used in this work? Is there a tonal center?
3. What melodic ideas are used and how are they treated? Is there a scale basis or consistent pitch patterning?
4. Analyze the texture of the "March." How does it compare to the texture of Copland's *Appalachian Spring*?
5. How does Persichetti establish "march" characteristics? What conflicts with the basic ¢ meter?

OTHER WORKS TO STUDY

Persichetti, Vincent: *Concerto for Piano, 4 Hands* (1952)
Piston, Walter: *Tunbridge Fair* (for Band) (1950)
Schuman, William: *Chester* (Overture for Band) (1956)

VINCENT PERSICHETTI

Divertimento for Band

SIXTH MOVEMENT, MARCH

10
15
Picc.
Fl. I II
Ob. I II
E♭ Cl.
I
B♭ Cl. II
III
Alto Cl.
Bass Cl.
Bsn. I II
Alto I II
Sax. Ten.
Bar.
Cor. I
II III
Trpt. I II
Hrn. I II
III IV
Euph.
Trbn. I
II III
Bass.
Timp.
S. D. W. B.
Cym. B.D.
a2
f marc.
ff
f
fp
mf
mp
W.W.
Brass
Percussion continues

20
25
Picc.
Fl. I II
Ob. I II
E♭ Cl.
B♭ Cl. I II III
Alto Cl.
Bass Cl.
Bsn. I II
Alto I II
Sax. Ten.
Bar.
Cor. I II III
Trpt. I II
Hrn. I II III IV
Euph.
Trbn. I II III
Bass.
Timp.
S.D.
W.B.
Cym.
B.D.
coll' 8va
20
25

30
Picc.
Fl. I II
Ob. I II
E♭ Cl.
B♭ Cl. I II III
Alto Cl.
Bass Cl.
Bsn. I II
Alto Sax. I II
Ten.
Bar.
Cor. I II III
a 2
Trpt. I II
Hrn. I II III IV
Euph.
Trbn. I II III
III
Bass.
Timp.
S.D.
W.B.
Cym.
B.D.
30
Bar., Tpt.
Hn., Sax.
Tbn.

35
40
Picc.
Fl. I II
Ob. I II
E♭ Cl.
B♭ Cl. I II III
Alto Cl.
Bass Cl.
Bsn. I II
Alto I II
Sax. Ten.
Bar.
Cor. I II III
Trpt. I II
Hrn. I II III IV
Euph.
Trbn. I II III
Bass.
Timp.
S.D. W.B.
Cym. B.D.
f marc.
W.W.

45
50
2nd time to Coda
Picc.
Fl. I II
Ob. I II
E♭Cl.
I
B♭ Cl. II
III
Alto Cl.
Bass Cl.
Bsn. I II
Alto I II
Sax. Ten.
Bar.
I
Cor. II III
Trpt. I II
Hrn. I II
III IV
Euph.
Trbn. I
II III
Bass.
Timp.
S. D. W. B.
Cym. B. D.
f
45
50
2nd time to Coda
Tpt.
f marc.

55
Picc.
Fl. I II
Ob. I II
E♭ Cl.
B♭ Cl. I II III
Alto Cl.
Bass Cl.
Bsn. I II
Alto I II
Sax. Ten.
Bar.
mf cresc. poco a poco
ff
Cor. I II III
Trpt. I II
Hrn. I II III IV
Euph.
Trbn. I II III
Bass.
a 2
Timp.
S. D.
W. B.
Cym.
B. D.
rim shot
f
W. W.
mf cresc. poco a poco
Tpt.
S.D.
Tbn.
ff

60
65
Picc.
Fl. I II
Ob. I II
E♭ Cl.
B♭ Cl. I II III
Alto Cl.
Bass Cl.
Bsn. I II
Alto I II
Sax. Ten.
Bar.
Cor. I II III
Trpt. I II
Hrn. I II III IV
Euph.
Trbn. I II III
Bass.
Timp.
S. D.
W. B.
Cym.
B. D.
ff
f
p cresc.
(f)
Timp.
Cym.
B.D.
S.D.
W.bl.
f Timp.

CODA
70
75
Picc.
Fl. I II
Ob. I II
E♭ Cl.
B♭ Cl. I II III
Alto Cl.
Bass Cl.
Bsn. I II
Alto I II
Sax. Ten.
Bar.
Cor. I II III
Trpt. I II
Hrn. I II III IV
Euph.
Trbn. I II III
Bass.
Timp.
S. D.
W. B.
Cym.
B. D.
ff marc.
a 2
W.W. coll' 8va bassa
W.W. coll' 8va
Brass
Cor., Tpt.

80
Picc.
Fl. I II
Ob. I II
E♭ Cl.
B♭ Cl. I II III
Alto Cl.
Bass Cl.
Bsn. I II
Alto I II
Ten. Sax.
Bar.
molto marc.
Cor. I II III
Trpt. I II
Hrn. I II III IV
Euph.
Trbn. I II III
Bass.
cresc.
a 2
Timp.
S. D.
W. B.
Cym.
B. D.
80
coll' 8va
molto marcato
+ all Perc.

MEL POWELL

1923, New York—

Mel Powell is one of a group of well-known younger American composers. He did work in composition at Yale University and has received a number of commissions and fellowships, including a Guggenheim Fellowship. Powell has written a variety of compositions for both electronic equipment and traditional instruments. He is presently chairman of the composition department and head of the electronic studio at Yale University.

FILIGREE SETTING FOR STRING QUARTET, 1959 (excerpt)

This composition is a one-movement work, half of which is reproduced on the following pages. It divides into a number of sections, which can be grouped as follows:

A	B	C	D	transition
pages 1-3	measures 1-21	measures 22-42	measures 43-57	measures 58-73

development of previous ideas and climax	A′
measures 74-138	pages 16-21

The composer has stated that the sections fall into a loose four-movement classical quartet scheme, condensed into one movement with interrelated sections.

The composition was premiered in August, 1960, at the Vancouver International Festival by the Claremont Quartet. It is one of the first compositions in which certain string effects (*e.g.,* finger drumming) are used.

1. Listen to the complete recorded work. Describe the sound possibilities of the string quartet that Powell has employed. Refer to the notes preceding the score in order to interpret the notation of the first three pages of score.
2. Listen to Powell's *Electronic Setting,* 1961, which is produced from electronic sources of sound. Compare the sounds used with the sounds employed by the string quartet in *Filigree Setting.*
3. Listen to *Filigree Setting* and discuss what creates a formal division before measure 1 (page 4) and at measures 22 and 43. Consider all the characteristics of sound. What other sectionalizing points can be found?
4. Study the pitch material of this composition to find unifying pitch patterns. For example, compare page 1, Violins I and II to measures 1-4, measures 22-24, and measures 43-46.
5. Listen to the whole work. Could various parameters of sound contribute to a different formal diagram than the one given here?
6. Compare the use of the instruments here to the other string quartets in this anthology.

OTHER WORKS TO STUDY

Berio, Luciano: *Differences* (1958-1960)
Brown, Earle: *Music for Cello and Piano* (1955)
Cage, John: *Sonatas and Interludes for Prepared Piano* (1946-1948)
Erb, Donald: *Sonata for Harpsichord and String Quartet* (1962)
Stockhausen, Karlheinz: *Refrain* (1959)

NOTES

I

calls for the wood of the bow to be bounced freely along the lengths of a specified pair of damped strings, thus engaging pitches in the course of its trajectory. On the violin or viola, the motion of the bow is directed from the bridge to the damping fingers near the nut. (Fingers rest in low first position, touching lightly as in the production of harmonics.) On the cello, the direction in which the bow is to be moved is specified in each instance.

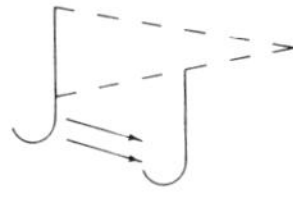

means the same bow stroke, with the bow crossing over at about the middle of the fingerboard from one pair of strings to another, as specified in each case.

calls for the very tip of the bow to be bounced along the length of a (specified) single string. Here, too, the fingers damp the strings. Sets of numbers placed beneath these symbols (*cf.*, also vc., score pg. 3) represent relative durational values, with a unit value chosen in each case by the individual player.

II

Finger drumming (on rib, table, etc.) is represented on one- or more-lined staffs as in the conventional notation of indeterminately pitched sound.

- ⌂ calls for drumming with fingernail *
- T stands for *thumb*
- F means *all fingers*

IV

X replaces a time signature where there are no fixed communal tempi and/or metrical units. In such cases, all parts begin simultaneously but thereafter each proceeds independently as directed.

Where points of entry must coincide in the course of such a section, the sign ⌐ appears, with the instruments involved specified.

The comma (,) calls for as short a pause as possible. Longer pauses are indicated by 𝄐, or 𝄐⋮ and their lengths are determined by the given cues for subsequent entries.

* To protect varnish, strips of thin tape or cellophane, adhesive though dry, may cover points at which finger-nails otherwise would contact the wood.

MEL POWELL

Filigree Setting for String Quartet (excerpt)

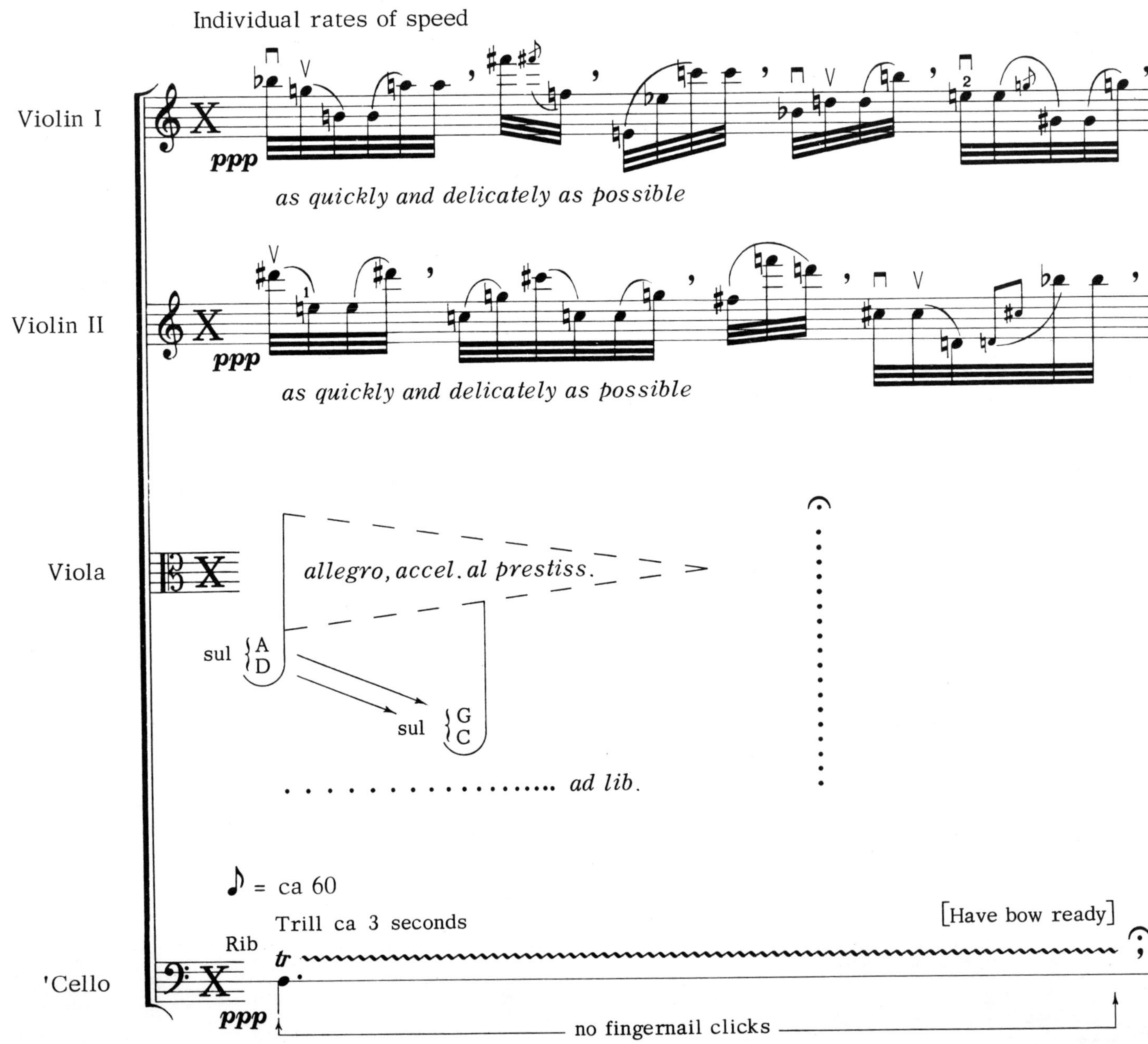

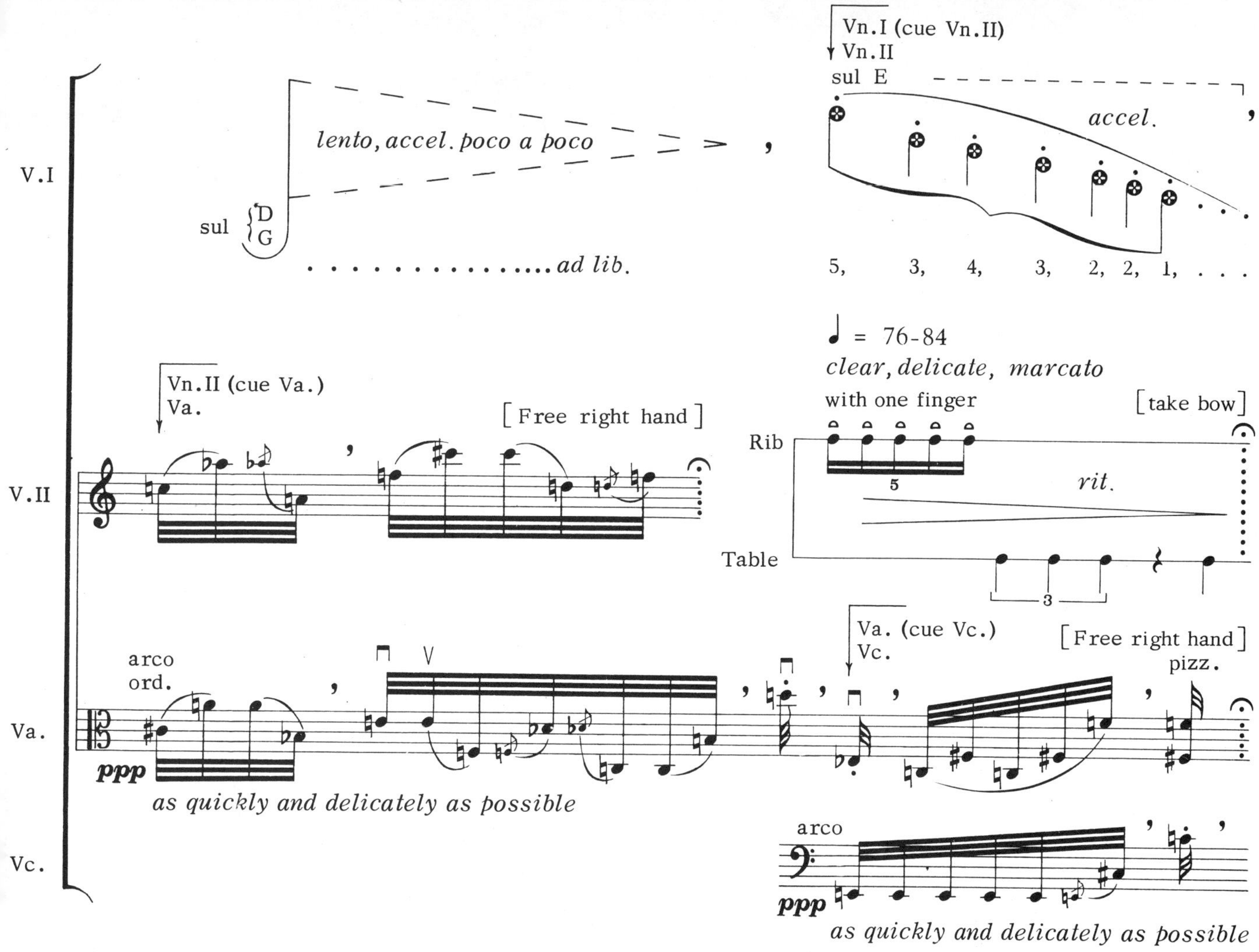

V.I

Vn.I (cue Vn.II)
Vn.II
sul E
accel.
5, 3, 4, 3, 2, 2, 1, . . .

sul {D G
lento, accel. poco a poco
. . . . *ad lib.*

V.II

Vn.II (cue Va.)
Va.
[Free right hand]

♩ = 76-84
clear, delicate, marcato
with one finger
[take bow]
Rib
rit.
Table

Va.

arco
ord.
ppp
as quickly and delicately as possible
Va. (cue Vc.)
Vc.
[Free right hand]
pizz.

Vc.

arco
ppp
as quickly and delicately as possible

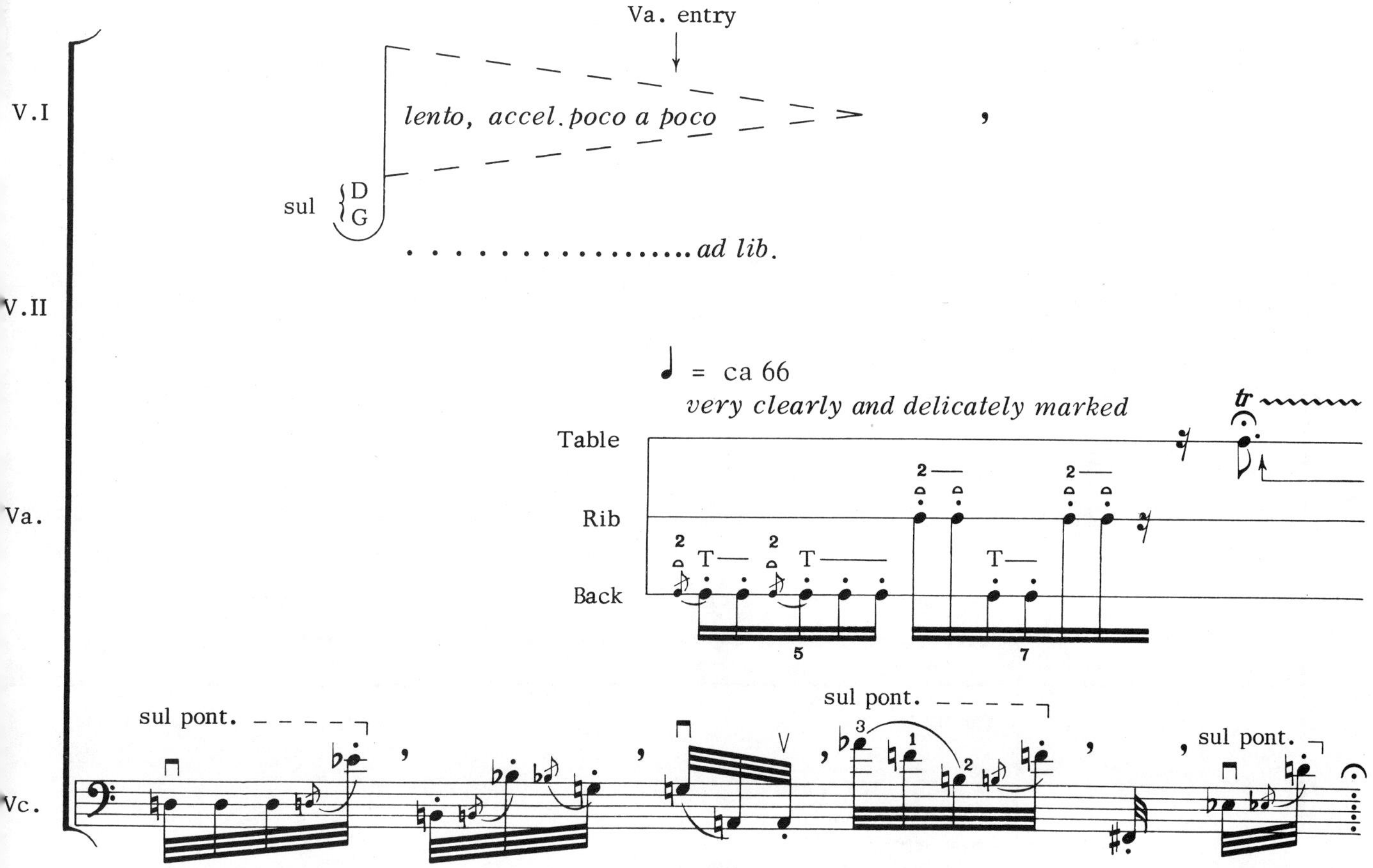

V.I

Va. entry
lento, accel. poco a poco
sul {D G
. . . . *ad lib.*

V.II

Va.

♩ = ca 66
very clearly and delicately marked
Table
Rib
Back

Vc.

sul pont.
sul pont.
sul pont.

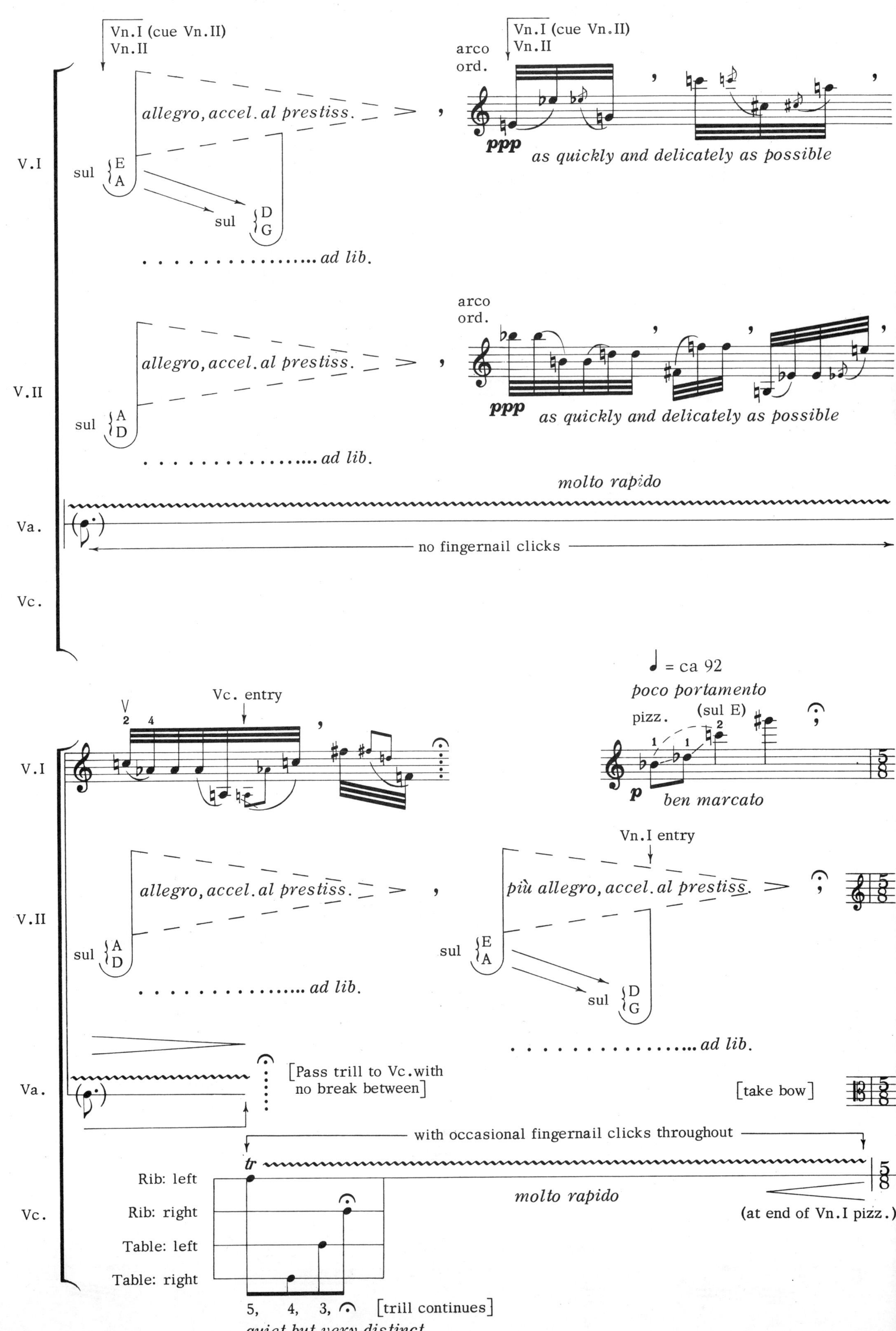

Vn.I (cue Vn.II)
Vn.II
allegro, accel. al prestiss.
sul E A
sul D G
ad lib.
arco
ord.
ppp
as quickly and delicately as possible
V.I
V.II
sul A D
molto rapido
Va.
no fingernail clicks
Vc.
Vc. entry
♩ = ca 92
poco portamento
pizz.
(sul E)
p
ben marcato
Vn.I entry
più allegro, accel. al prestiss.
[Pass trill to Vc. with no break between]
[take bow]
with occasional fingernail clicks throughout
tr
Rib: left
Rib: right
Table: left
Table: right
(at end of Vn.I pizz.)
5, 4, 3,
[trill continues]
quiet but very distinct

= 126
arco
arco
Rib: right
marc.
arco
pizz.
arco
ricochet
arco ord.
col legno
pizz.
arco
pizz.
molto
pizz.
pizz. with fingernail
arco

poco rit.
sul pont.
8
arco
pizz.
9
arco
arco ord.
sul tasto
pizz.
ricochet
sim.
ricochet
sim.
pizz.
a tempo
10
11
12
arco
leggierissimo
pizz.
arco
arco (G) (C)
sul tasto
col legno
pizz.
col legno
pizz.
poco f, secco
(sim.)
Agitato, pressando
13
14
15
cresc.
cresc.
cresc.
col legno
arco ord.
piu f

accel.
Subito giusto
(a tempo: ♪= 126)
pizz.
arco
poco flautando
pesante
leggiero
sul pont.

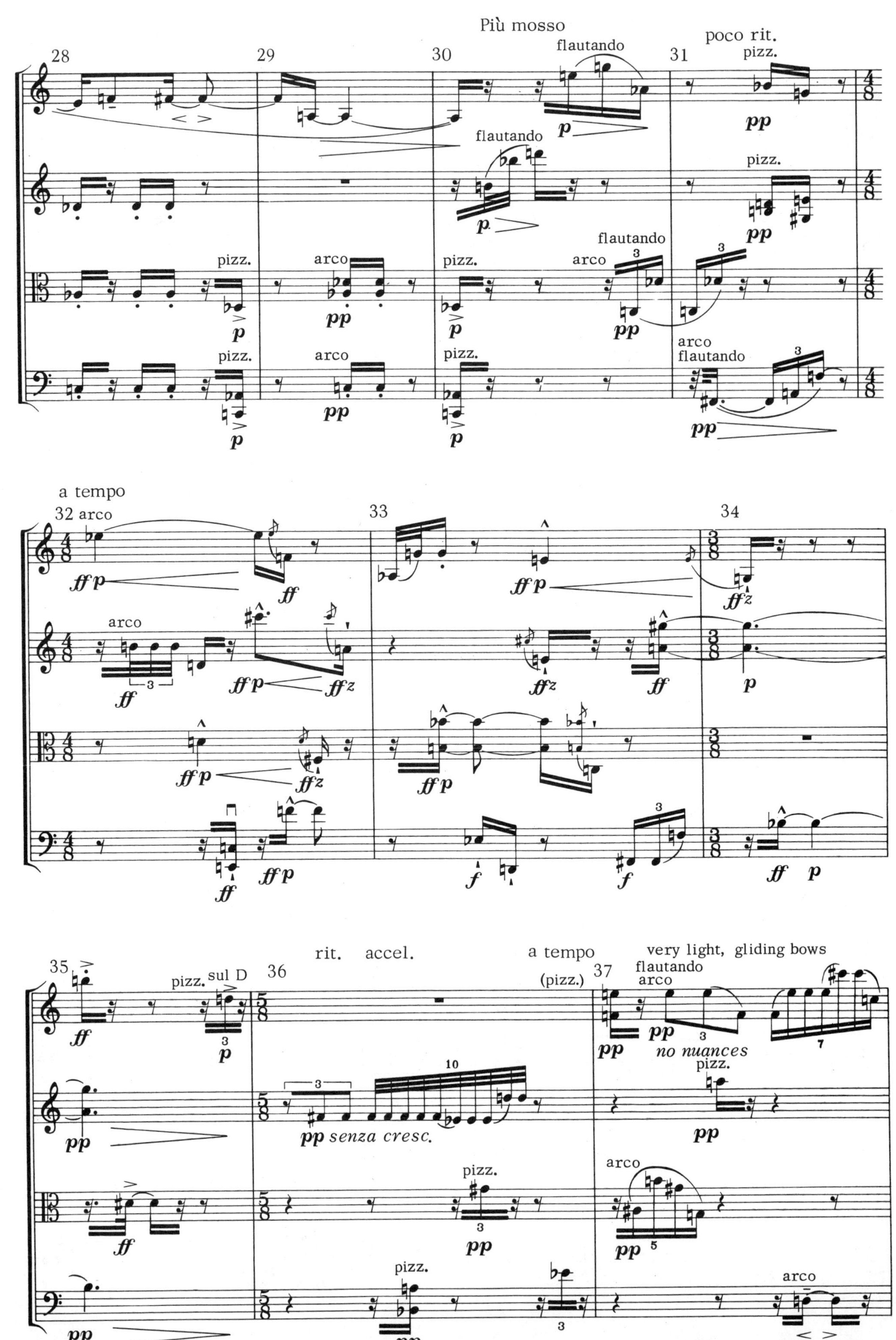
Più mosso
flautando
poco rit.
pizz.
flautando
pizz.
pizz.
arco
pizz.
arco
flautando
pizz.
arco
pizz.
arco
flautando
a tempo
32 arco
33
34
arco
35
pizz. sul D
36
rit. accel.
a tempo
(pizz.)
37
very light, gliding bows
flautando
arco
no nuances
pizz.
pp senza cresc.
pizz.
arco
pizz.
arco

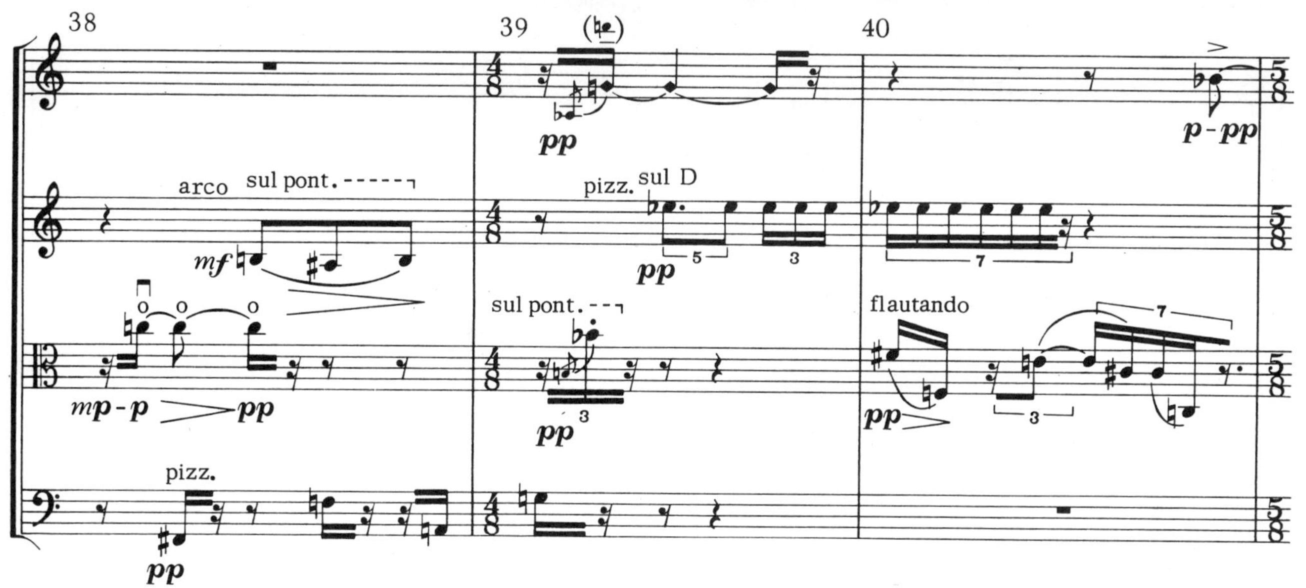

38
39
40
arco
sul pont.
mf
mp-p
pp
pizz.
pp
pizz. sul D
pp
5
3
sul pont.
pp
3
p-pp
7
flautando
pp
3
7

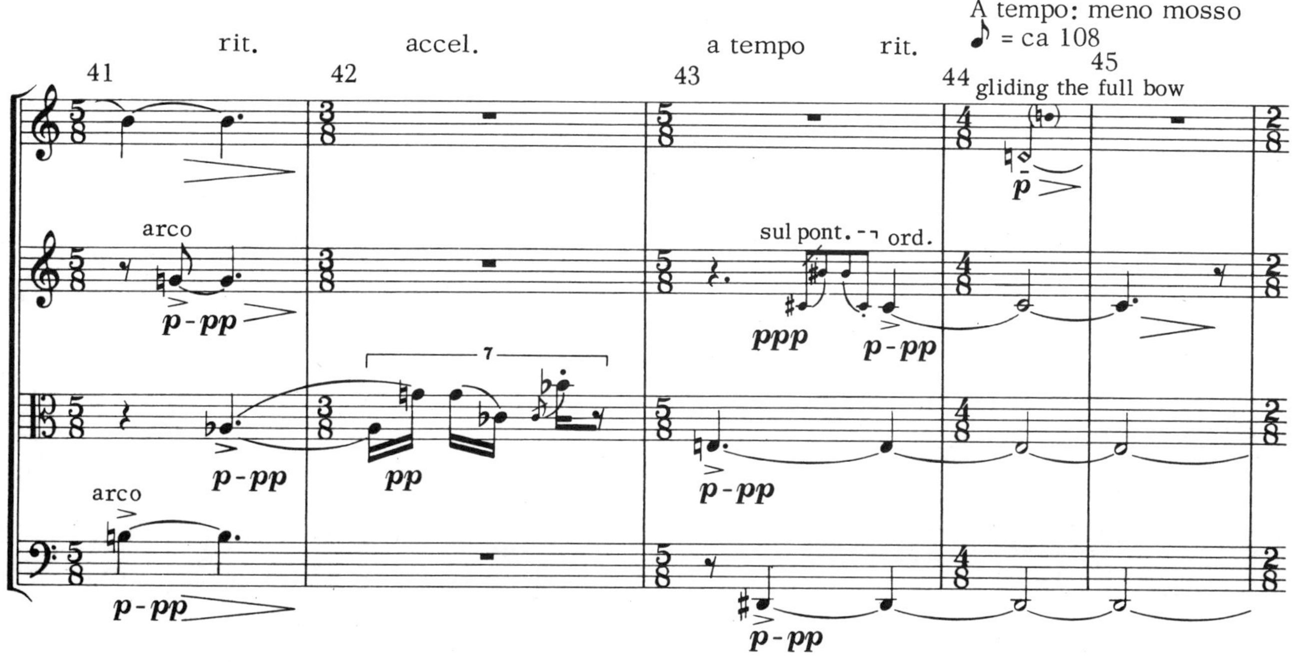

rit.
accel.
a tempo
rit.
A tempo: meno mosso
♪ = ca 108
41
42
43
44
45
gliding the full bow
p
arco
p-pp
sul pont. ord.
ppp
p-pp
7
p-pp
pp
p-pp
arco
p-pp
p-pp

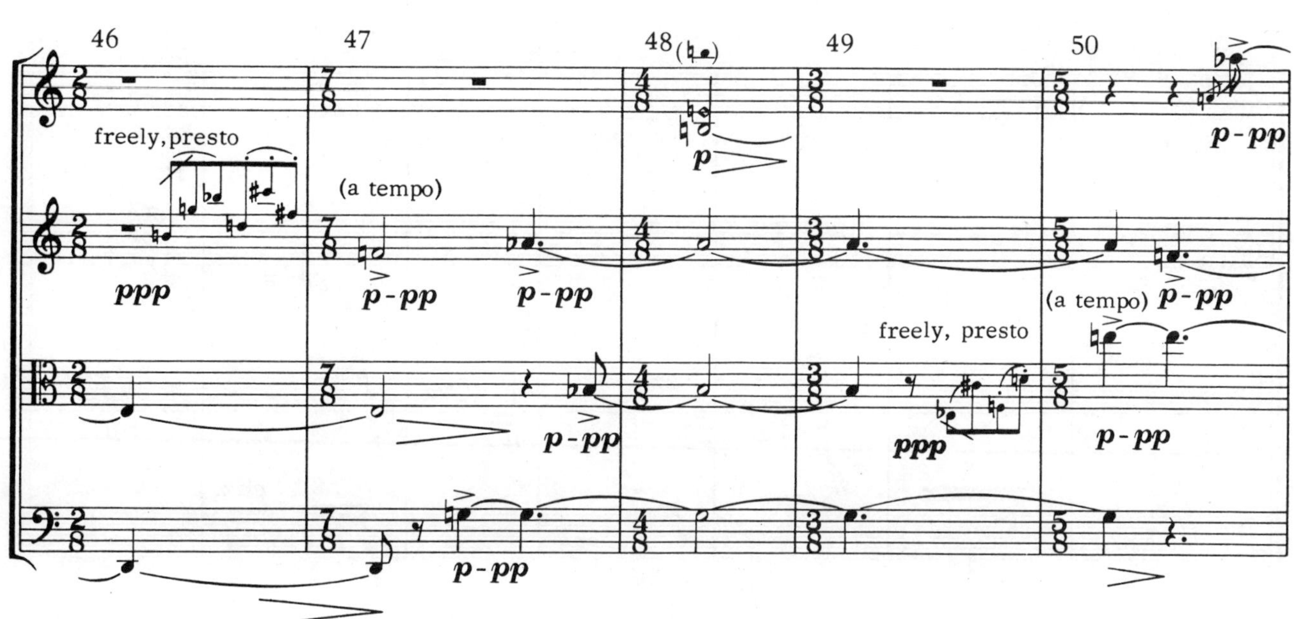

46
47
48
49
50
p
p-pp
freely, presto
ppp
(a tempo)
p-pp
p-pp
(a tempo) p-pp
freely, presto
p-pp
ppp
p-pp
p-pp

poco meno mosso
a tempo
poco meno mosso
accel.
espr.
espr.
espr.
p espr.
rit.
a tempo
flautando
rit.
a tempo
accel. Tempo: ♪= 138
sul tasto
flautando
leggiero
sul pont.
p espr.
pizz.
(8va)
pizz.
pizz.
arco
arco
pizz.
arco
pizz.
arco
pizz.
arco
pizz.

ARNOLD SCHOENBERG

1874, Vienna—1951, Los Angeles

Arnold Schoenberg was a Viennese composer who has greatly influenced composition in the twentieth century. His work was an outgrowth of the late German romantic tradition of Bruckner and Mahler; together with his pupils Webern and Berg, Schoenberg expanded this tradition to include new tonal and expressionistic possibilities. Schoenberg's work is varied, spanning all of the first half of the century.

The composer is perhaps best known for his development of a serial technique of composition, where a pre-compositional pitch arrangement (row) is used as the basis for the pitch material. Two of the works below are serial; one is not. In spite of their differences in compositional technique, they have similarities in the treatment of intervals, chords, and rhythms. Study these musical aspects first before concentrating on the serial manipulations.

SIX SHORT PIECES FOR PIANO, Op. 19, 1911

These pieces are not serial but illustrate the development of a free atonal style that is rooted in nineteenth-century tonality. They represent Schoenberg's early period of composition and are his most compressed compositions. The six pieces show an extreme concentration of thought. The second of the set is reproduced here.

1. Trace the third as a constructive element in this piece.
2. How do the terms "tonality" and "form" apply to this piece?
3. Compare this piece and others in Op. 19 to Berg's *Songs,* Op. 2 and to Webern's *Orchestra Piece,* Op. 6, reproduced in the anthology.

ARNOLD SCHOENBERG

Six Short Pieces for Piano, Op. 19

NO. 2

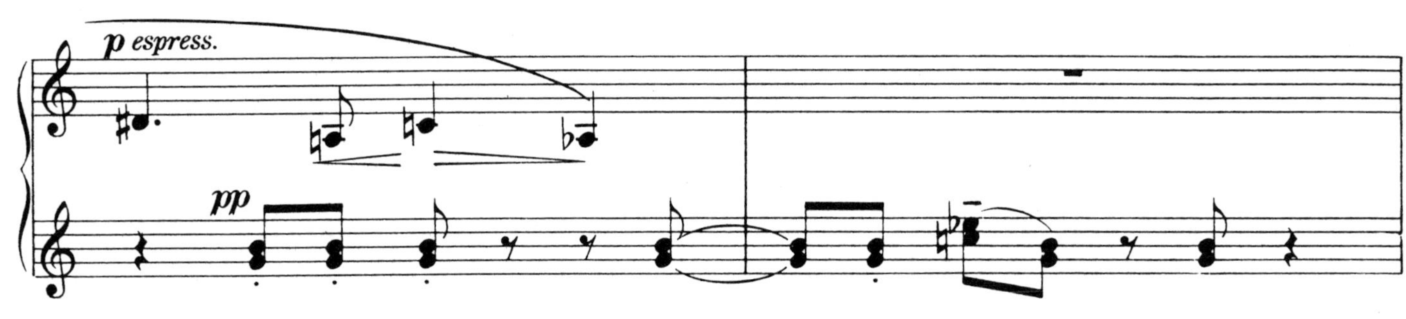

Schoenberg, SUITE FOR PIANO, Op. 25, 1925

This suite is Schoenberg's first complete serial composition. It consists of six movements, of which the Gavotte and Musette are the second and third. (The Gavotte is repeated after the Musette, in the manner of a Baroque dance suite.) The suite is based on the following twelve-tone row:

Gavotte and Musette

1. What elements create division into phrases and motives? Look for cadence patterns, sequences, rhythmic and pitch repetitions, etc.
2. What factors, other than a reuse of the pitch row, unify these pieces?
3. How is the twelve-tone row used in these pieces? Find examples of melodic lines and sonorities constructed from the row or its permutations. How is the row divided into parts?
4. The movements of the suite have titles similar to the movements of Baroque suites. How do these pieces justify the titles "Gavotte" and "Musette"?
5. What is the role of rhythm and meter? Compare rhythmic elements here to those in other piano compositions in the anthology.

ARNOLD SCHOENBERG

Suite for Piano, Op. 25

GAVOTTE

10
p dolce
p dolce
dolce
rit.
dim.
15
dolce
Ped.
tempo

fp
sf
fp
20
f
sf
p
f
f
25
p
sf
fp
sf
rit.
f
ff
ff
attacca

MUSETTE

Rascher (𝅗𝅥 = 88)
fp
fp
f
ff
f
pp
5
ff
f
p
sf
sf
sf
accel.
rit.
a tempo
pp
fp
pp
sf
sf

10
pp
pp
p
Ped.
accel.
f
pp
f
8
rit.
15
ff
p
p
f
Ped.
poco rit.
pp
6
p
sf

tempo
pp
pp
sf
ppp
molto legato
sf
sf
sf
sf
pp
sf
pp
sf
sf
sf
pp
p
f
p
f
f
p.
sf
mf
sf
sff
sf
sf
accel.
rit.
fp
sf
pp
sf
ppp
Gavotte da capo

Schoenberg, VARIATIONS FOR ORCHESTRA, Op. 31, 1928

This composition consists of an introduction, theme, nine variations, and a finale. It is a serial composition based on a row stated in the theme by the cellos. The introduction is an "anticipatory" variation of the melodic and harmonic material presented in the theme. Op. 31 is a good example of the deft compositional interaction of a tone row with Schoenberg's particular melodic, harmonic, and rhythmic ideas.

Introduction, Theme, and Variation One

1. Study the theme (measures 34-57) and notate the tone row (found in its original form in the cello line). How does the cello line present the row in the course of the theme?
2. Study the "accompaniment" in the theme. What kinds of sonorities are used? How is the accompaniment related to the tone row?
3. What contributes to phrasing in the theme?
4. What variational procedures are applied in Variation I?
5. How is the Introduction related to the material presented in the theme? Analyze melodic lines, harmonic structures, and the emergence of the tone row.
6. The motive, B A C H, found in the trombone in measures 24-25, becomes very important in the course of the work, especially in the finale. Analyze measures 24-25 for uses of the tone row.
7. Listen to the whole composition and describe the variational techniques used. Listen for the treatment of material presented in the Introduction and Theme. Analyze at least one other variation in detail for use of the tone row, of melodic materials, of textures used, etc.

OTHER WORKS TO STUDY

Schoenberg, Arnold: *Five Pieces for Orchestra,* Op. 16 (1909)
Pierrot Lunaire, Op. 21 (1912)
String Quartet No. 4, Op. 37, I (1936)
Concerto for Violin and Orchestra, Op. 36, II (1936)
Survivor from Warsaw, Op. 46 (1947)

ARNOLD SCHOENBERG

Variations for Orchestra, Op. 31

INTRODUCTION

etwas drängend
Fl 1. 2.
Ob 1.
Kl 1.
Bs Kl
Fg 1.
Hr 2.
m Dpf
m Dpf
Hrf
etwas drängend
I. Gg
II. Gg
Br
Vcl
Kbs
pizz
(pizz)
arco
etwas drängend

Fl 1.2.3.
Ob 1.2.3.
E H
Es Kl
Kl 1.
Fg 1.2.3.
Hr 1.2.3.4.
m Dpf
Trp 1.
Hrf
Cel
I. Gg
II. Gg
Br
Vcl
Kbs
14
15
16
17
18
a 3
a 4
m Dpf
o Dpf
pizz
arco

𝅗𝅥. = 𝅗𝅥 (des 3/2) und = 𝅗𝅥. (des 12/8)
steigernd
19
20
21
pesante
22
Pic
Fl 1.2.3.
1.2.
Ob
3.
E H
Es Kl
Kl 1.2.3.
Bs Kl
Fg 1.2.3.
KFg.
1.3.
Hr.
o Dpf
2.4.
Trp 1.2.
o Dpf
1.2.
Pos
3.4.
Tª
Tamt
gestopft
a 2
a 3
pizz
I. Gg
II. Gg
Br
Vcl
Kbs
(G)
steigernd
pesante

rit . . . . . . Tempo I; wieder ruhig
𝅗𝅥. = 𝅗𝅥 des Tempo I = 60
1. Fl 2.3.
p leicht
pp
fp
Ob 2.3.
E H
sfp
pp
f
1. Kl 2.3.
p
pp dolce
a 2
Bs Kl
Fg 1.
offen
1. Hr 3.4.
Pos 1.
pp dolce
Cel
m Dpf
3 fach get
I. Gg
II. Gg
Br
Vcl
pizz
arco
p dolce
dolce

29
30
31
32
33
Pic
Fl 1. 2. 3.
a 3
pp
Ob 1.
p
pp
E H
Es Kl
ppp
Hr 1. 2.
m Dpf a 2
o Dpf
Trp 1.
m Dpf
Hrf
I. Gg
m Dpf
(m Dpf)
ppp
II. Gg
m Dpf
Br
pizz
arco
Vcl
Flag
Kbs

Molto moderato (♩= 88)
Ob 1.
E H
Kl 2.
Fg 3.
Hr 2. o Dpf
Hrf
Vcl
Kbs
p zart
poco rit . . . .
Bs Kl
Hr 1.2.
eventuell KFg

poco rit
Ob 1.
E H
Kl 2.
Bs Kl
Fg 3.
Hr 1. 2.
Hrf
I. Gg
m Dpf
Vcl
Kbs
(m Dpf)
pp sehr ruhig
pp dolce
o Dpf
poco rit
pp sehr ruhig
pp dolce

VARIATION I

Moderato (♩= 72)
58
59
60
61
Pic
Fl 1.
Ob 1.2.
cantabile
a 2
E H
Es Kl
Kl 1.2.
Bs Kl
Fg 1.2.3.
a 3
KFg
Hr 1.2.
Trp 1.2. o Dpf
p dolce
Hrf
Cel
Moderato (♩= 72)
(arco) get
p stacc
I. Gg o Dpf
II. Gg o Dpf
pizz
Br
cantabile
Vcl
Kbs
Moderato (♩= 72)

Pic
Fl 1.
Ob 1.2.
E H
Es Kl
Kl 1.2.
Bs Kl
Fg
KFg
Hr 1.2.
Trp 1.2.
Hrf
Cel
I. Gg
II. Gg
Br
Vcl
Kbs
a 2
espress
p dolce
1. pizz
2. arco
get
alle arco
mp stacc

65
66
67
68
Pic
Fl 1.
Ob 1.2.
Es Kl
Kl 1.
Bs Kl
Fg 1.2.3.
KFg
Hr 1.2.
Trp 1.2.
Pos 1.4.
Hrf
Cel
Xyl
I.Gg
II.Gg
Br
Vcl
Kbs
p
f
mf
ff
mf dolce
cantabile
pcantabile
espress
mf dolce

69
rall. . . . . . :70
71
72
Fl 1.2.3.
a 3
Ob 1.
E H
Kl 1.
espr
Bs Kl
Fg 1.2.3.
a 3
KFg
1. 2.
Hr
3 4.
p dolce
3. m Dpf
m Dpf
m Dpf
m Dpf
a 2
a 2
1.
Trp
2. 3.
m Dpf
p cantabile
m Dpf
o Dpf
1. 2.
Pos
3. 4.
2. m Dpf
3. m Dpf
o Dpf
o Dpf
Hrf
69
rall. . . . . . :70
71
72
I. Gg
II. Gg
get pizz
Vcl
3 fach get pizz
unis arco
get
Kbs
69
rall. . . . . :70
71
72

73
74
75
76
Pic
espress
Fl 1.2.3.
a 3
1.
Ob 1.2.
a 2
Es Kl
Kl 1.
Bs Kl
Fg 1.2.3.
KFg
1.3.
Hr
m Dpf
2.4.
1.3. o Dpf
2.4. o Dpf
1.
o Dpf
Trp
2.3.
m Dpf
Pos 1.2.
o Dpf
Hrf
Cel
Glsp
I. Gg
II. Gg
unis
arco
Vcl
Kbs

calando......
77
78
79
80
81
Pic
Fl 1.2.3.
1.2.
Ob
3.
E H
Es Kl
1.
Kl
2.3.
Bs Kl
Fg 1.2.3.
KFg
1.3.
Hr
o Dpf
2.4.
1.
o Dpf
Trp
2.3.
m Dpf
1.2.
Pos
3.4.
Tª
Pk
a 2
a 3
(hart)
o Dpf
I. Gg
II. Gg
Br
Vcl
Kbs
pizz
(pizz)
arco
attacca
81 calando.......

GUNTHER SCHULLER

1925, New York—

Gunther Schuller, a prominent American composer, was self-taught in composition. Schuller began his musical career by playing French horn with a number of important orchestras. An increasing number of commissions led him to leave playing in 1959 and devote himself to composition, conducting, and teaching. The composer is well known for a successful opera, chamber works, and orchestral pieces. He has been a professor at Tanglewood and Yale. Presently he is head of the New England Conservatory in Boston.

In addition to his work in classical music, Schuller has worked with the Modern Jazz Quartet and has produced compositions in the jazz idiom. He is a contributing editor to *Down Beat* and has written on the history of jazz. He has also been identified with a "third stream" which combines classical and jazz elements, a combination which has been popular throughout the twentieth century. The piece reproduced here represents this "third stream" movement.

SEVEN STUDIES ON THEMES OF PAUL KLEE, 1959

This set of seven pieces was commissioned in 1959 by the Ford Foundation and the Minneapolis Symphony. Schuller selected seven pictures by Paul Klee as inspirations for the seven studies; the studies are a "retranslation into musical terms of the 'musical' elements in certain Klee pictures." The picture entitled "Little Blue Devil" evoked a jazz idiom with "blue" instrumental colorings. It is the third in the set and is reproduced here.

The orchestral score is not reduced, as all instruments sound as written and in many places the scoring is quite thin. Some of the effects (percussion) cannot be reproduced on the piano. A reduced version could be played by piano, percussion, bass, and a melody instrument.

III, Little Blue Devil

1. Listen to the piece without the score. Describe the texture and general form. Consider instrumental groups, densities, interaction of parts, melodic and rhythmic material.
2. Listen again with the score. Study the melody. What is the basic melodic material? What happens to this material in the course of the composition?
3. Play through the solo contra-bass line. Are there recurring patterns? What intervals are used? How does this line function in the texture?
4. Compare the contra-bass line, the other melodic material, and the chordal structures. Are there any pitch (interval) relationships? Is there any application of a serial technique?
5. What importance do rhythm and meter have in this piece?
6. What "jazz" elements are used in this piece? Listen to other jazz and third stream compositions and compare the materials and techniques used (*e.g.*, Modern Jazz Quartet *Third Stream Music, Outstanding Jazz Compositions of the Twentieth Century*). In addition, find other classical composers who have used jazz or popular elements in their music.

OTHER WORKS TO STUDY

Schuller, Gunther: *Music for Brass Quintet* (1961)
Concertino for Jazz Quartet and Orchestra (1959)
Foss, Lukas: *Echoi,* II and III (1963)

GUNTHER SCHULLER

Seven Studies on Themes of Paul Klee

III, LITTLE BLUE DEVIL

5
Cym.
S. D.
brushes
Vns.
pizz.
arco
Va.
Vc.
pont.
Cb.
I Solo
pizz. sul D
gliss.
10
A
Fl.
Ob.
E. H.
Cls.
B. Cl.
Bns.
Hns.
Tpts.
Tbns.
Cym.
S. D.
Sock Cym.
Sock Cym.
10
A
Vns.
pizz.
Va.
pizz.
Vc.
pizz.
Cb.
I Solo
gliss.

Hns. 1 2 3 4
Tpt. 1
Cym. 2
Sock Cym.
Cb.
con sord.
15
Cup mute
I Solo
poco dim.
20
Cym. 1 2
B
a 2
Fls. 1 2
senza sord.
brushes
S. D.
25

Fls.
Hns.
Tpt.
Cym.
Sock Cym.
Vns.
Va.
Vc.
Cb.
I Solo
30
Cls.
Tbns.
Harp
C
35
a 2
con sord.
3. con sord.
Cup mutes
arco
mf
mp
p
f

Fls. 1 2
poco marc.
Obs. 1 2
E. H.
Cls. 1 2
a 2
mp
B. Cl.
mp
Bns. 1 2
Cbn.
Hns. 1 2
mf
3 4
Tpt. 1
(opt. legato-tongued)
poco marc.
Tbns. 1 2
mf
mp
3
mf
mp
Tuba
Cym. 2
Sock Cym.
Harp
mp
Vns. 1
p
2
p
Va.
p
Vc.
I Solo
Cb.
I Solo

40
Fls. 1 2
Obs. 1 2
E. H.
Cls. 1 2
B. Cl.
Bns. 1 2
Cbn.
Hns. 1 2 3 4
Tpt. 1
Tbns. 1 2 3
Tuba
Cym. 2
Sock Cym.
Harp
Vns. 1 2
Va.
Vc.
Cb.
a2
I Solo
pizz.
mf
mp

D
Fls.
Obs.
E.H.
Cls.
B.Cl.
Bns.
Cbn.
Hns.
Tpts.
Tbns.
Tuba
I. senza sord.
open
open
Vib.
motor on, no pedal
Cym. 2
Sock Cym.
Harp
D
Vns.
Va.
Vc.
Cb.
I Solo

45
Fls. 1 2
Obs. 1 2
I.
E. H.
Cls. 1 2
B. Cl.
Bns. 1 2
Cbn.
Hns. 1 2 3 4
Tpts. 1 2 3
Tbns. 1 2 3
Tuba
Vib.
Cym. 2
Sock Cym.
Harp
45
Vns. 1 2
Va.
Vc.
Cb.
on the string
I Solo

Meno mosso ♩ = ca. 72
50
Fls. 1 2
Obs. 1 2
I.
E. H.
Cls. 1 2
lazy triplets
B. Cl.
Bns. 1 2
Cbn.
Hns. 1 2 3 4
Tpts. 1 2 3
Tbns. 1 2 3
Cup mute
lazy triplets
Tuba
Vib.
Cym. 2
Sock Cym.
Harp
Vns. 1 2
ff furioso
Va.
Vc.
Cb.
I Solo

a tempo
Fls.
Obs.
E. H.
Cls.
B.Cl.
Bns.
Cbn.
Hns.
Tpts.
Tbns.
Tuba
Vib.
Cym. 2
Sock Cym.
Harp
a tempo
Vns.
Va.
Vc.
Cb.
I Solo

E 55
Fls. 1 2 3
Obs. 1 2
E.H.
Cls. 1 2
B.Cl.
Bns. 1 2
Cbn.
Hns. 1 2 3 4
Tpts. 1 2 3
Tbns. 1 2 3
Tuba
Vib.
Cym. 2
Sock Cym.
Harp
E 55
3 Soli
poco vibr.
others pizz.
Vns. 1 2
Va.
Vc.
poco vib.
pizz.
others
1 Solo
Cb.
più p
mp sub.

60
Fls. 1 2 3
pp
pp
p
Obs. 1 2
E. H.
Cls. 1 2
pp
B. Cl.
pp
Bns. 1 2
Cbn.
Hns. 1 2 3 4
(Cup mute)
mp
f
Tpts. 1 2 3
Tbns. 1 2 3
Tuba
Vib.
mp
f
Cym. 2
Sock Cym.
Harp
mp
mf
p
60
tutti
Vns. 1 2
mf
tutti
mf
3 Soli
Va.
(pizz.)
p
others
mf
p
3 Soli
pizz.(unis.)
mp
Vc.
others
(pizz.)
mf
p
1 Solo
Cb.

rit.
Molto meno mosso e pesante ♩= ca. 54
poco rit.
F 65
a tempo
Fls.
Obs.
E. H.
Cls.
B. Cl.
Bns.
Cbn.
Hns.
Tpts.
Tbns.
Tuba
Glsp.
Vib.
Cym. 2
Sock Cym.
Fl. 3 change to Picc. I
senza sord.
a 2
open
3. con sord.
gliss.
Cup mute
Vns.
Va.
Vc.
Cb.
tutti
arco
3 Soli
others
tutti div. a 3
I Solo
div. 1/2 arco
1/2 pizz.

Fls.
Cl.
Tpt.
Cym.
Sock Cym.
Vns.
Va.
Vc.
Cb.
I Solo
70
Fl.1 change to Picc.3
Fl.2 change to Picc.2
mp
Picc.
75
dim.
p
più dim.
ppp
p più dim.
pp

G
Picc.
Ob.
Cls.
Bns.
con sord.
Hns.
Tpts.
Tbns.
brush, tight from edge gradually to center
Susp. Cym. I
dim.
ppp
Vns.
div.
Va. div. a 3
senza vibrato
Vc. div. a 3
I Solo
gliss.
2 players
slow gliss.
Cb.

IGOR STRAVINSKY

1882, Oranienbaum, Russia—

Igor Stravinsky is one of the most famous of twentieth-century composers. Born near St. Petersburg, Stravinsky studied law at the university there and met Rimsky-Korsakov, who had a strong influence on his early writing. Stravinsky's early ballets, produced by Diaghilev in Paris, established the composer's importance early in the twentieth century, and since then Stravinsky has been an influential figure.

Stravinsky's creative work has spanned more than two-thirds of the twentieth century and has encompassed a range of styles, from his glittering orchestral scores of the 1910's and the more compact, neo-classic style of the 1920's and 1930's to the serialism and less immediate style of the 1950's and 1960's. Throughout all his writing, however, Stravinsky maintains similar compositional processes and materials; only the context changes. The excerpts below span Stravinsky's writing from 1911-1955 and illustrate a small part of this very prolific composer's output. *Petroushka* (1911) is one of the early ballets; *L'Histoire du Soldat* (1918) is another stage work, much reduced in scope. *In Memoriam Dylan Thomas* (1954) is an early serial work and *Canticum Sacrum* (1955) is a larger serial work composed for St. Mark's in Venice.

PETROUSHKA, 1911

Together with *Fire Bird* and *Rite of Spring, Petroushka* forms a group of three famous ballets composed by Stravinsky between 1910 and 1913. *Petroushka's* plot centers around a showman and his three puppets: Petroushka, the comic-pathetic clown (Pierrot); the Moor; and the Ballerina. The puppets perform for a carnival crowd in St. Petersburg and subsequently play out their own drama. The Moor and Petroushka fight and the clown is killed.

In the "Russian Dance," from the end of the first tableau, the puppets come to life and perform a Russian dance, much to the astonishment of the crowd. The excerpt is reproduced here in the full orchestral score and in a reduction on three staves. The reduction is not for piano performance but shows the various orchestral layers and simplifies analysis. It can be played in sections on one piano and completely on two pianos. The second piano should play the middle staff from measure 9 to 35, the bottom staff from measure 59 to 70, the middle staff from measure 71 to 88, and the bottom staff from measure 112 to the end. Stravinsky and others have arranged solo piano or two piano versions of this dance.

Russian Dance

1. Listen to the dance without the score and diagram formal sections. What creates form? Listen for various elements (melodic material, dynamics, orchestration, etc.). Then study the score and diagram separately the form created by each parameter.
2. Notate the melodic and rhythmic material used in the dance. What characteristics does the material have? What processes are used to extend the basic material?
3. Study the orchestration in detail. How does Stravinsky create unity and variety through orchestration? Compare this orchestration to other works in the anthology.
4. Study the chords used in the excerpt. What sorts of sonorities are employed? Is there a key center or any changes of center? Compare harmony and tonality here to these elements in the Persichetti "March" in the anthology.

IGOR STRAVINSKY

Petroushka

RUSSIAN DANCE

34
10
Fl. Picc. I. II.
Fl. I. II.
Ob. I. II. III.
Cor. Ingl.
Cl. I. II.
Cl. III.
Fag. I. II.
Fag. III.
Cor. I. II.
Cor. III. IV.
Pist. I. II.
Trgl.
Tamb. de Basque
Xyloph.
Arpa I.
Arpa II.
Piano.
2 V. Soli.
V. I.
V. II.
3 sole
Viole
le altre
Celli
I.
a 2.
I. II.
III.
I. Solo
mf sempre grottesco
con sord.
I. Solo marcato
gliss.
m.d.
m.g.
arco pp sempre
arco
pizz.
div. pizz.
sub. meno f
poco
sempre - simile
sf sub. meno f
marc.
mf sempre grottesco
sf sub. meno f
simile

15
Fl. Picc. I.
Fl. I.II.
a 2.
Ob. I.
Solo
stacc.
Cl. I.
Solo
Pist. I.
simile
Trgl.
Tamb. de Basque
Xyloph.
Arpa I.
Arpa II.
Piano
2 V. Soli
V. I.
gli altri
arco
pizz.
V. II.
sf sub. meno f
3 sole
Viole
le altre
sf sub. meno f
Celli
sf sub. meno f
marc.
sf sub. meno f

20
35
25
Fl. Picc. I. II.
Fl. I. II.
Ob. I. II
Cor. Ingl.
Cl. I. II.
Cl. III.
Fag. I.
Fag. II. III.
Cor I
Pist. I. II.
Tr. I. II.
Xyloph.
Arpa I.
Arpa II.
Piano
2 V. Soli
Vni I. gli altri
V. II.
3 sole
Viole
le altre
Celli div.
C. B.
p stacc.
p sub. stacc.
poco più f
p sub.
p poco marc.
sempre stacc.
pp stacc. leggiero
mf leggiero
tutti stacc.
arco
arco tutte
pizz.
sim.

36
crescendo sempre 30
Fl. Picc. I. II.
Fl. I. II.
Ob. I. II.
Cor. Ingl.
Cl. I. II.
Cl. III.
Fag. I.
Fag. II. III.
Pist. I. II.
Tr. I. II.
Xyloph.
Arpa I.
Arpa II.
Piano.
V. I.
V. II.
Viole.
Celli.
cresc.
a 2.
sempre stacc.
crescendo sempre
crescendo sempre 30
36
crescendo sempre 30

35
37
a 2.
Fl. Picc. I. II.
Fl. I. II.
Ob. I. II. III.
I. II.
I. II. III.
Cor. Ingl.
Cl. I II.
Cl. III.
Fag. I.
Fag. II. III.
Cor. I. II.
poco
Cor. III. IV.
Pist. I. II.
Tr. I. II.
Xyloph.
gliss.
Camp.
Arpa I.
Arpa II.
Solo
Piano.
gliss. poco a poco accel.
V. I.
div.
V. II.
Viole.
stacc.
Celli.
arco
C. B.

38
40
Fl. Picc. I. II.
Fl. I. II.
Ob. I. II. III.
Cor. Ingl.
Cl. I. II. III.
Fag. I. II. III.
Cor. I. II.
Pist. I. II.
Tr. I. II.
Xyloph.
Camp.
Arpa I.
Solo
sol #
Arpa II.
Piano.
V. I.
V. II.
sf
Viole.
f
Celli.
C. B.

39
45
50
Fl. Picc. I. II.
Fl. I. II.
Ob. I. II. III.
Cor. Ingl.
Cl. I. II. III.
Fag. I. II. III.
Cor I. II.
Pist. I. II.
Tr. I. II.
Xyloph.
Camp.
G. Cassa.
Piatti.
Arpa I.
Arpa II.
Piano.
V. I.
V. II.
Viole.
Celli.
C. B.
(a 2.)
a 2.
I. Solo
II. Solo
II. III.
I. II.
III.
I.
II.
mf
ff
sff
meno f
poco marc. ma p
come sopra
modo ordinario
pizz.
gliss.
p sub.
p
f
+ 8

40
55
Fl. Picc. I. II.
Fl. I. II.
Ob. I. II.
I. Solo.
Cor. Ingl.
Cl. I. II.
Cl. III.
Fag I.
Solo
Fag II.
Solo
Fag III.
meno f
Cor. I. II.
Pist. I. II.
Tr. I. II.
G. Cassa.
Piatti.
Piano.
V. I.
2 V-ni Soli
arco
scherzando
leggiero
V. II.
simile
pizz.
cresc.
Viole.
simile
Celli.
unis.
meno f
C. B.

41
60
Cor. Ingl.
Cl. I. II.
3 Cl. = in la
Cl. III.
Fag. I.
Fag. II.
Arpa I.II.
a 2.
Piano.
m. d.
scherzando
leggiero
8 V-ni Soli
Gli altri. V. I.
pizz.
V. II.
Viole
Celli.

Fl. Picc. I.
Fl.gr.I.
I. II.
Cl. (La)
III.
Piatti.
Triang.
Arpa I.
Piano.
V.I.Tutti.
V. II.
Viole.
65
scherzando
modo ordinario
pizz.
m.d.

Fl.gr.I.
I. II.
Cl. (La)
III.
Arpa I.
Piano.
V. II.
Viole.

70
42
Fl.gr.I.II.
I. II.
Cl.(La)
III.
3 Cl. in si♭.
I. II.
Corni.
III. IV.
poco sf sub. p
sempre simile
Arpa I.
Piano.
pp sub.
V. solo.
mf scherzando
V. II.
Viole.
mf
pp sub.
poco sf sub.p
simile

Ob. I.
I. II.
Cl. (sib)
III.
Cl. basso. (sib)
Corni.
Piano.
V. solo.
75
80
Solo.
mf
p
simile

poco a poco cresc.
85
Fl. Picc. I.
Fl.gr. I.II.
Ob. I.II.
Cl. I. II.
Cl III.
Cl. basso.
Fag. I.
Fag. II.
Xyloph.
Piano.
V. solo.
simile
I.
a 2.

90
95
Poco meno (tranquillo)
pochiss. accel.
a tempo
rall.
Fl.gr.I.II.
Ob.I.II.
Cor. Ingl.
Solo.
simile
Cl.I.II.III.
I.Solo.
Cl.basso.
Fag.I.II.
I. II. Corni. III. IV.
poco
pizz.
V.I.
V.II.
Viole.
Celli.
C.B.
43
Tempo I. (Allegro giusto.)
100
con sord.
Tr. I.
Piano.
f subito
Tempo I. (Allegro giusto)
f sub.

Fl. Picc. I. II.
Fl. gr. I. II.
Ob. I. II.
Cor. Ingl.
Cl. I. II.
Fag. I. II.
Tr. I.
Piano.
V. I.
V. II.
Viole.
Celli.
105
a 2.
I. II.
ten.
legato
pizz.
arco

44
110
115
I.
a 2.
Fl. Picc. I.II.
Fl.gr. I. II.
I. II.
Ob.
III.
Cl.I.II.
Fag.I.II.
Tr. I.
Arpa I.
Piano.
V. I.
V. II.
Viole.
Celli.
(pizz.)
(arco)
pizz.
arco

Fl. Picc. I. II.
Fl.gr. I. II.
I. II.
Ob.
III.
Cl.I.
Cl.II.III.
Fag.I.
Fag.II.III.
Cor.I.II.III.
Cor.IV.
Tr. I.II.
Xyloph.
Arpa I.
Arpa II.
Piano.
V.I.
V.II.
Viole.
Celli.
C.B.
120
45
a 2.
unis.
arco
pizz.
div.

125
46
cresc. ed accel.
a 2.
Fl. Picc. I. II.
Fl. gr. I. II.
I. II.
Ob.
III.
Cl. I.
Cl. II. III.
Fag. I.
Fag. II. III.
Cor. I. II. III.
Cor. IV.
Tr. I. II.
Xyloph.
Arpa I.
Arpa II.
Piano.
V. I.
V. II.
Viole.
Celli.
C.B.
arco
unis.
pizz.
div.

Для окончанія
Pour finir
130
Fl. Picc. I. II.
Fl. gr. I. II.
I. II.
Ob.
III.
Cl. I.
Cl. II. III.
Fag. I. II. III.
a 2.
4 Corni.
I. II.
III. IV.
Pist.
Tr. I. II.
Trb. I. II.
Trb. III. e Tuba.
Xyloph.
Timp.
G. Cassa.
Arpa I.
Arpa II.
Piano.
V. I.
V. II.
Viole.
Celli.
C. B.
div.
pizz.
unis.
arco

Stravinsky, L'HISTOIRE DU SOLDAT, 1918

The Soldier's Tale, composed in 1918, is a stage work to be narrated, acted out, and danced. The narration, which forms part of "The Soldier's March" and the "Great Chorale" sections quoted on the following pages, is eliminated here. (Narration occurs during solo ostinato passages and fermate in these sections.) The suite from *The Soldier's Tale* consists of several short pieces, beginning with "The Soldier's March" and ending with the "Chorale" and the "Triumphal March of the Devil." A number of melodic fragments bind the work together, and characteristic rhythmic and timbral elements recur throughout. The suite illustrates Stravinsky's style of writing around 1920 and also shows the influence of popular music (specifically ragtime) on much music of this era. For a concrete example, see the three dances in the suite: "Tango," "Waltz," and "Ragtime."

The Soldier's March, Great Chorale, and Triumphal March of the Devil

1. Listen to the whole suite. Note melodic, rhythmic, and instrumental features which recur.
2. Study "The Soldier's March." What rhythmic characteristics are present in this excerpt? How are pulse and meter established or negated?
3. Notate the melodic material used in this first movement. What characteristics does it have (range, intervals used, patterns, etc.)? Trace this material through the movement and through the rest of the suite.
4. Sing each line of the "Great Chorale." Compare these lines to those of a Bach chorale.
5. Study the sonorities of the chorale. What chords are used? What cadence chords are used?
6. Diagram the instrumentation used throughout the chorale. Listen to the effect of different placements of the instruments. How do spacing and instrumentation affect the balance of the lines?
7. Listen to the "Triumphal March of the Devil" without the score and diagram the form. What elements return and what provides contrast?
8. What processes does Stravinsky use to create form in the "Triumphal March"? Compare form in this march with form in the *"Russian Dance"* from *Petroushka.*
9. Compare the formal and the rhythmic procedures in this last movement to the first movement of the suite ("The Soldier's March").
10. Compare the use of instruments here with instrumentation in the other Stravinsky works reproduced in the anthology.

IGOR STRAVINSKY

L'Histoire du Soldat

THE SOLDIER'S MARCH

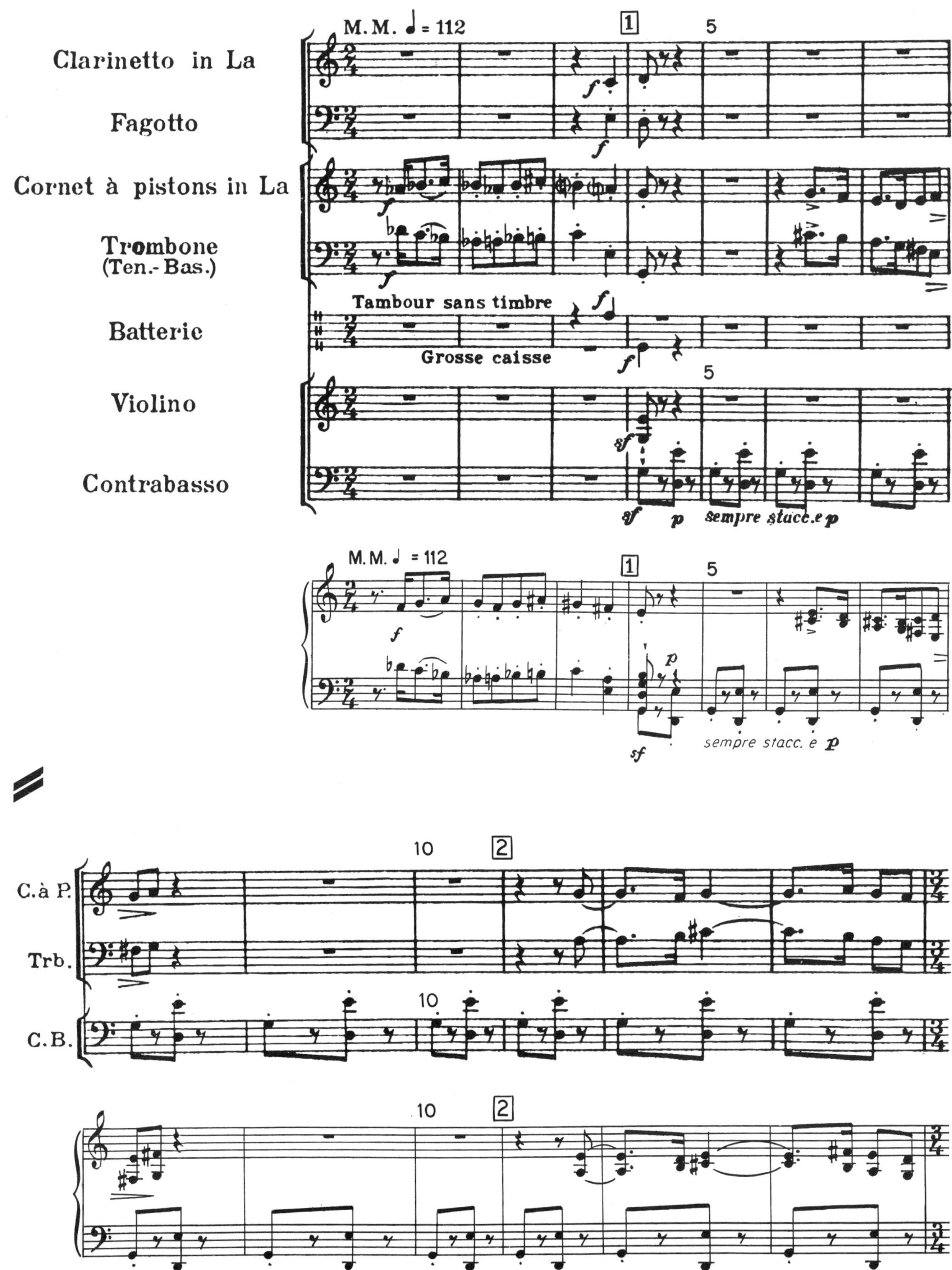

15 [3] 20

Fg. p

C.à P. poco sf > e sub. p

Trb.

15 20

Vl. pizz. sf

C.B. pizz. sf

15 [3] 20

p sub. p sf

=

[4] 25

Cl. sf sub. dim.

C.à P. mf

Trb. f 25

Vl. arco sf pizz.(non arpeg.) sf

C.B. arco (con sopra) poco sf p

[4] 25

f sf dim. mf

sf p (♮)

5 30

Cl.

Fg.

C.à P.

Vl.

C.B.

mf stacc.

p

Solo

mf

30 arco jeté

f

5 30

mf stacc.

p

f

mf

35

Cl.

Fg.

C.à P.

Vl.

C.B.

(Solo)

mf

p sub.

p sub.

poco più f

jéte

35

35

p sub.

6
40
Cl.
Fg.
C.à P.
Vl.
C.B.
simile
jeté
mf
f
poco sf
7
45
Tamb. de Basque
Caisse claire sans timbre, grande taille
Grosse Caisse
Batt.
pizz

8
50
55
Cl.
Fg.
C.à P.
Trb.
Batt.
*)
f
mf
arco
sempre
non
arpeg.
etc.
Vl.
C.B.
più f

9
60
Cl.
Fg.
ff
C.à P.
Trb.
Batt.
Vl.
sub. meno f
C.B.
9
60
ff
sub. meno f

10
Solo
65
70
Cl.
Fg.
Trb.
T.de B.
C.cl.
Gr.C.
sempre simile
p sub.
Vl.
stacc.
C.B.
11
75
C.à P.
sempre stacc.

12 80 13

Cl.

Fg.

Solo

pp sub.

C. à P.

Trb.

T. de B.
C. cl.
Gr. C.

80

Vl.

p sub.

C. B.

p

12 80 13

pp sub.

p sub.

85 14

Cl.

mf

Fg.

poco cresc.

85

Vl.

simile

C. B.

85 14

mf

90
15
Cl.
Fg.
C.à P.
Trb.
C.cl.
Gr. C.
Vl.
C.B.
mf
mp
p
lunga ad libit.
Drums ad lib.

GREAT CHORALE

2
10
Cl.
Fg.
C.à P.
Trb.
Vl.
C.B.
mf
p
poco cresc.
sub. meno f
3
15
Pist.
mp
lunga ad lib.

4
Cl.
Fg.
Pist.
Trb.
Vl.
C. B.
pp
mp
lunga ad lib.
p
sul Ré
lunga ad lib
p lunga ad lib.

TRIUMPHAL MARCH OF THE DEVIL

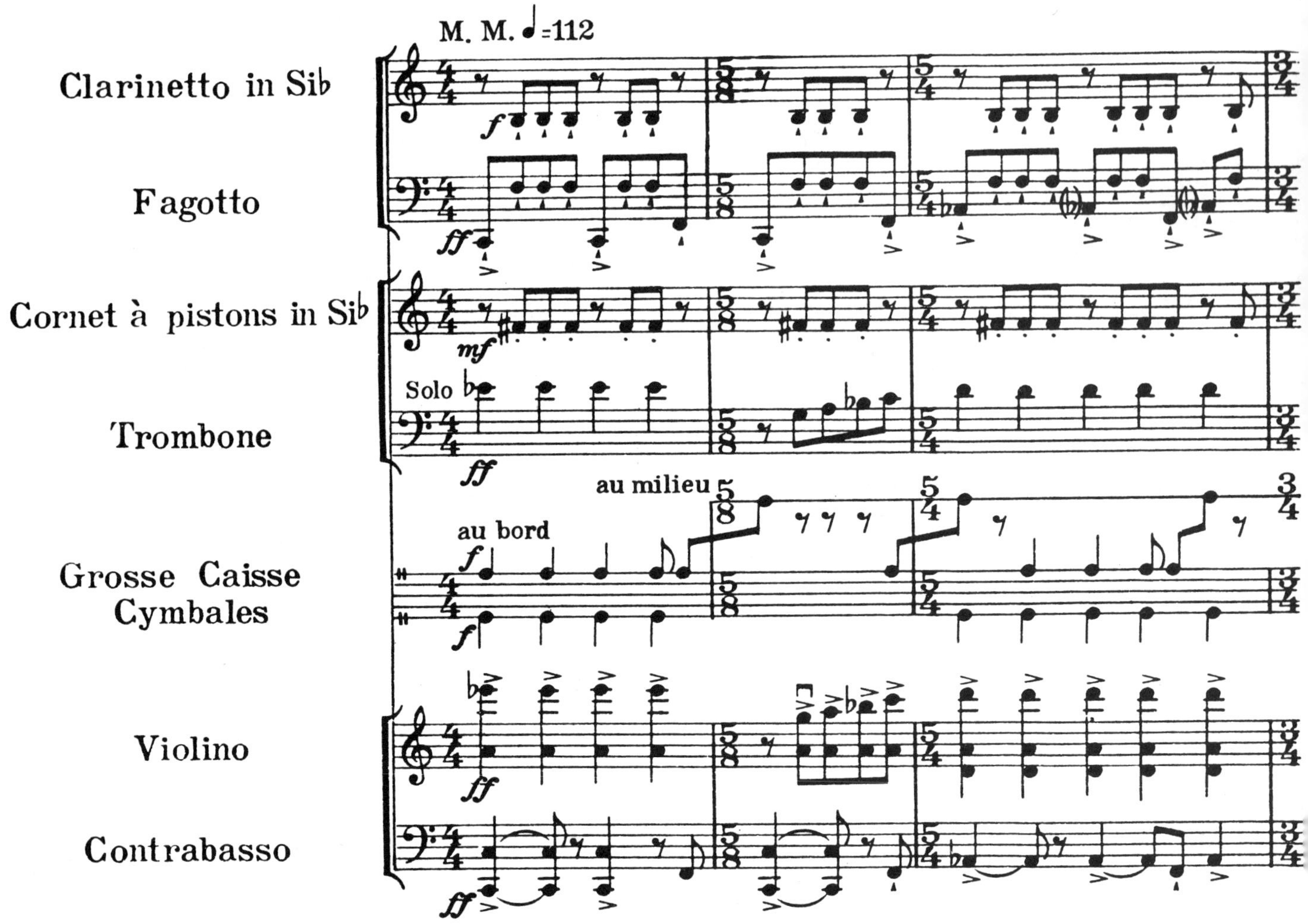

M. M. ♩=112
Clarinetto in Sib
Fagotto
Cornet à pistons in Sib
Trombone
Grosse Caisse
Cymbales
Violino
Contrabasso
Solo
au milieu
au bord
f
ff
mf

1
5
C. à P.
Trb.
Vl.
C. B.
Solo
f
(très court, du talon)
très sec
très sec

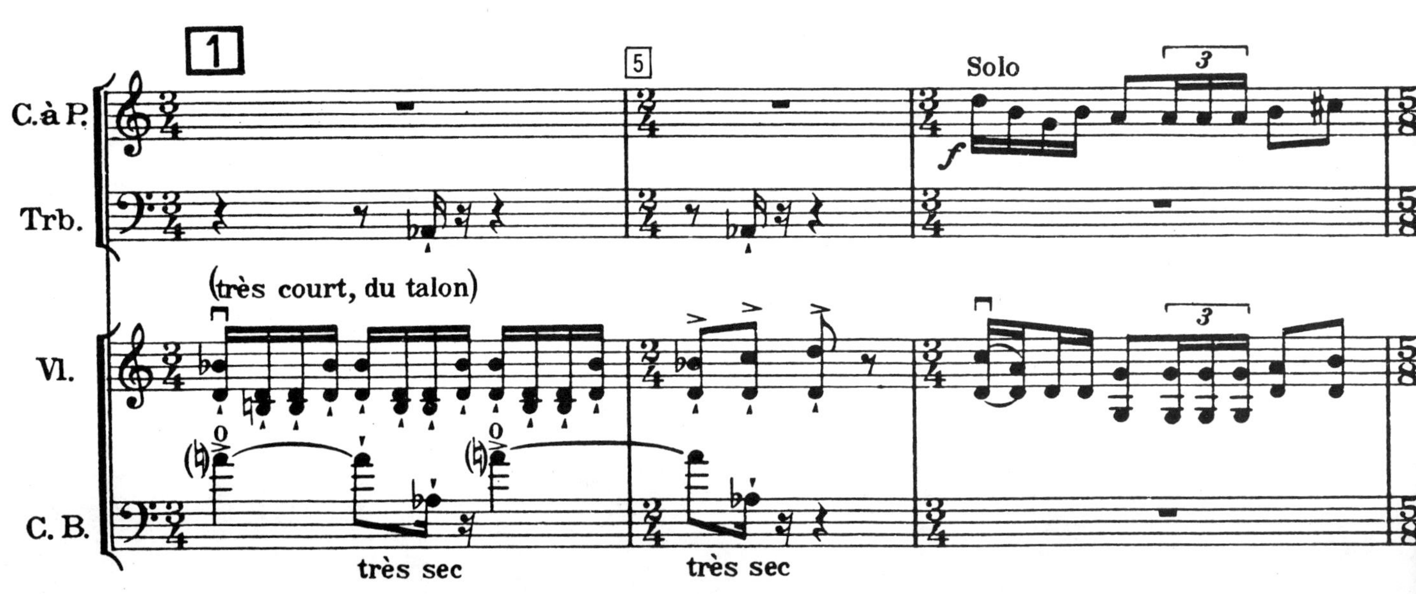

C. à P.
Ossia
Trb.
più sf
Tamb. et 2 C. cl.
Les queues en haut pour la m. d., les queues en bas pour la main gauche.
Bag. à feutre dur
petite
forte
Gr. C.
Vl.
C. B.
poco sf (secco)
secco assai
Cl.
Fg.
simile
etc. sim.
Solo
(mailloche)
Cymb.

20
Tamb. et 2 C. cl.
gr.
Petite
Gr. C.
Vl.
sf
25
Tamb. et 2 C. cl.
Gr. C.
Vl.
sf
sf
30
4
Cl.
ff
Fg.
C. à P.
f
Solo
Trb.
ff
Tamb. et 2 C. cl.
Gr. C. au bord
au milieu
Gr. C. Cymb.
f
Vl.
ff
30
C. B.
ff

35
5
Tmb.
et
2 C.cl.
Gr.C.
Vl.
sf
(♭)
stacc.
C.à P.
Tmb.
et
2 C.cl.
Gr.C.
mf
Vl.
ten.
ten.
40
6
Cl.
f
f
Fg.
f
ff
C.à P.
mf
Solo
Trb.
ff
Tmb.
et
2 C.cl.
Gr.C.
au bord
Gr.C.
40
Vl.
sf
sf
ff
C.B.
ff

45
7
Cl.
Fg.
C.à P.
Trb.
sf
au milieu
Gr.C.
Cymb.
(très court, du talon)
45
Vl.
C.B.
très sec
Solo
f
8
50
ossia
Trb.
poco sf
Tmb. et 2 C.cl.
Les queues en haut pour la m.d., les queues en bas pour la m.g.
Baguettes à feutre dur
Gr.C.
Vl.
C.B.
poco sf (secco)

Trb.
Tmb. et 2 C.cl.
forte
Gr.C.
Vl.
C.B.
secco assai
sf
55
9
f
stacc.
60
65
10
70

11
Tmb. et 2 C.cl.
Gr.C.
Vl.
12
75
Cl.
Fg.
C.à P.
mf
f
ten.
ten.
sf
13
80
Trb.
poco sf
ff
p
bag. à tête en feutre dur
stacc.
C.B.

85
Tamb. et 2 C.cl.
Gr. C.
Vl.
sf
15
90
16
95
100
17
Le rideau tombe lentement
Der Vorhang fällt langsam
The curtain falls slowly
Cl.
Fg.
C. à P.
pp
105
110
Fin

Stravinsky, IN MEMORIAM DYLAN THOMAS, 1954

In Memoriam Dylan Thomas was composed soon after the death of the poet in 1953. Stravinsky chose Dylan Thomas's poem "Do not go gentle into that good night" as the central section of the piece and set it for tenor voice and string quartet. This section is surrounded by a Prelude and Postlude entitled "Dirge-Canons," set for quartets of strings and trombones. The Prelude is reproduced here.

The work is one of Stravinsky's early serial compositions and is interesting because of its use of a five-tone row, instead of the more usual twelve-tone row. The composition was completed in 1954.

Dirge-Canons (Prelude)

1. Find the five-tone row and trace it completely throughout the excerpt. What processes does Stravinsky apply to the row?
2. Study the cadence points of the excerpt. Is there any tonal focus? What sonorities are used at cadences?
3. What creates form in this excerpt? What is the justification for the title "Dirge-Canons"?
4. Compare the Prelude with the Postlude as to tonality, cadences, form, and treatment of the row.
5. Compare this work to the "Great Chorale" of *L'Histoire du Soldat.* What are the similarities and the differences in the lines and the sonorities used?
6. After studying Stravinsky's melodic lines in other pieces, why is this five-tone row a logical choice for a serial composition? Compare this serial work with the Schoenberg *Variations for Orchestra,* Theme, and the Webern *Cantata.*
7. Study the song following the Prelude. How is the row used here?

IGOR STRAVINSKY

In Memoriam Dylan Thomas

DIRGE—CANONS (PRELUDE)

C
15
D
Trb. ten.
Trb. bo.
Vln. 1
Vln. 2
Vla.
Vc.
come sopra
p
marc. ma p
20
1'27"
pp
attacca sub.

Stravinsky, CANTICUM SACRUM, 1955

Canticum Sacrum was composed as a tribute to the city of Venice, in praise of its patron, Saint Mark. The ensemble, including chorus, tenor and baritone soloists, winds, brass, strings, and organ, is Venetian in character and makes use of opposing bodies of sound. *Canticum Sacrum* has five sections and an opening dedication and is arranged in an arch shape: Section V is an exact retrograde of Section I; Sections II and IV are solos; and Section III is a central presentation of the three virtues (Charity, Hope, Faith). Serial procedures are used in Sections II, III, and IV.

Section II, the tenor solo, is reproduced here.

II, Surge, aquilo

Surge, aquilo; et veni, auster;
perfla hortum meum, et fluant aromata illius.
Veniat dilectus meus in hortum suum,
et comedat fructum pomorum suorum.
Veni in hortum meum, soror mea, sponsa;
messui myrrham meam cum aromatibus meis;
comedi favum meum cum melle meo;
bibi vinum meum cum lacte meo.
Comedite, amici, et bibite;
et inebriamini, carissimi.

Awake, O north wind; and come, thou south;
blow upon my garden, that the spices thereof may flow out.
Let my beloved come into his garden,
and eat his pleasant fruits.
I am come into my garden, my sister, my spouse;
I have gathered my myrrh with my spice;
I have eaten my honeycomb with my honey;
I have drunk my wine with my milk;
Eat, O friends; drink,
yea, drink abundantly, O beloved.

Vulgate, Song of Songs, IV, 16, V.

1. Sing the vocal line and study it for its structure: intervals used, melodic patterns, phrases and cadences, contour, tonal centers, etc. What repetitive elements are there? How is the line developed? Compare it to the vocal lines of the Berg *Songs* and the Webern *Cantata.*
2. Find the twelve-tone row in operation here. How is the row used to provide chords or lines? Compare serial procedures here to those in *In Memoriam Dylan Thomas.*
3. Study the instrumentation of this movement. What unifying elements are there? What contrasting elements?
4. Listen to the whole *Canticum Sacrum* and discuss timbres and textures used.

OTHER WORKS TO STUDY

Stravinsky, Igor: *Le Sacre du printemps* (1913)
Octet for Wind Instruments (1923)
Symphony of Psalms (1930)
Symphony in Three Movements (1945)
Mass (1948)
Movements for Piano and Orchestra (1958-1959)

IGOR STRAVINSKY

Canticum Sacrum

II, SURGE, AQUILO

Ten.
Fl.
Arpa
Ve - ni - at... di - lec - tus me - us in hor - tum su - um, et co - me - dat fructum po - morum su - o - rum......
Fltr.
Bb Db Eb
dolce assai
Ve - ni, ve - ni in hor - tum me - um, so - ror me - a, spon - sa;..
cantabile
Fltr.
A♮ Gb Fb
Db
F♮ G#
B♮
etc. stacc.
dolce
.... mes - su - i myr - rham me - am, ... mes - su - i myr -
A#
C#
harm.
suoni reali
harm.
- rham, myr - rham .... me - am cum a - ro - ma - ti - bus me - is;....... co -

80
81
82
83
Ten.
Fl.
Arpa
3 C'bas. Soli
- me-di fa-vum me-um cum mel-le me - - - o;......
bi-bi vinum meum cum lac-te
suoni reali
suoni reali
84
85
86
87
88
C.I.
me - - - o..........
Co-me-di-te, co-me-di-te, a-mi-ci,...
et bi-bi-te;....
ppp
G♮ A♭
come sopra
come sopra
89
90
91
poco rit.
92
93
et i-ne-bri-a-mi-ni, i - ne-bri - a - mi-ni, ca - ris - si - mi.................
G♭
loco
A♮

ANTON WEBERN

1883, Vienna—1945, Mittersill, Austria

Webern's music is usually discussed in conjunction with that of Berg and Schoenberg and placed in the "New Viennese" school. Webern was a research musicologist and received a Ph.D. in 1906 from the University of Vienna. He was a pupil of Schoenberg and held various conducting positions. His mature years were spent in semi-retirement in Mödling, composing and teaching. He was mistakenly shot and killed at the end of the Second World War.

Webern's music moves from an expanded tonal style, typical of the German late romantic composers, to the very concentrated expression of ideas in his late works. Webern adopted the serial approach to composition and his works reveal one of its strictest applications; his compositions are often constructed out of a balanced row and utilize symmetrical architectural designs. In addition, Webern has influenced many other composers by his pointillistic approach to color: basic ideas of one to four notes are tossed between a number of instruments. The compositions on the following pages include one of the *Six Orchestra Pieces,* Op. 6, illustrating an early free atonal style, and the first movement of one of Webern's late works, *Cantata,* Op. 29, illustrating a compact, balanced, serial style.

SIX PIECES FOR ORCHESTRA, Op. 6, 1909

This set of six pieces for orchestra is dedicated to Arnold Schoenberg, "teacher and friend" and was first performed in 1913.

No. 1, Langsam

1. Listen to the first piece without the score. Diagram the piece according to texture and dynamics.
2. Study the melodic lines. How are they constructed? Compare the melodic material to the *Cantata,* Op. 29.
3. What elements create unity in this movement? What creates contrast?
4. Compare this piece to Schoenberg's Op. 19, No. 2 and Berg's Op. 2, quoted in this anthology. What similarities of musical material and techniques are there? What differences?
5. Listen to all of Webern's Op. 6 and discuss the shape of each movement. Consider all parameters (texture, melodic lines, dynamics, rhythm, chords, etc.).

ANTON WEBERN

Six Pieces for Orchestra, Op. 6

NO. 1

5
6
7
8
1.2.Fl.
1.2.Ob.
1.Kl.in B
B.-Kl.in B
1.2.Fg.
1.2.
Hr. in F
3.4.
1.Trp.in B
Hfe
1.
Gg.
2.
Br.
Vlc.
Cb.
a2
p dim.
a2 mit Dmpf.
dim.
mit Dmpf.
SOLO am Steg
ALLE (mit Dmpf.)
SOLO
sfp cresc.
p dim.
cresc.

9
10
11
12
1.2.Fl.
sf
P dim.
1.2.Ob.
sf
1.2.Kl.in B
a2
f
P
B.-Kl.in B
sf
1.2.Fg.
sf
2. nimmt Contrafg.
1.2.
Hr. in F
3.4.
sf
dim.
Dmpf. ab
1.
Trp. in B
2.3 4.
a 3 mit Dmpf.
f
P dim.
p dim.
1.
Gg.
2.
ohne Dmpf.
f
P dim.
Br.
Vlc.
sfp
Cb
mit Dmpf.
p dim.

rit.
1.2.Fl.
1.2.Kl.in B
dim.
offen
ged.
1.
Hr.in F
4.
mit Dmpf.
1.
Trp.in B
2.3.4.
Cel.
gliss.
Hfe
1.
Gg.
2.
pizz.
Br
gel.
Vlc
arco
Cb.

Webern, CANTATA, Op. 29, 1940

This composition is a three-movement one for chorus, orchestra, and soprano solo, first performed in 1946. It is based on a twelve-tone row made up of only three intervals. The row is so constructed that the retrograde and retrograde-inversion forms duplicate the inverted and original forms.

The text of the first movement is given below.

Zundender Lichtblitz des Lebens schlug ein aus der Wolke des Wortes. Donner der Herzschlag folgt nach, bis er in Frieden verebbt.	Lightning, the kindler of Being, struck, flashed from the word in the storm cloud. Thunder, the heart beat, follows, at last dissolving in peace.
Hildegard Jone	English version by Eric Smith

First Movement

1. Listen to the movement and note the orchestration used. How are the lines distributed among the instruments and the chorus?
2. Study the voice parts in measures 14-19. Four statements of the row are presented here. Determine the row and the relationships of the four rows to each other. What kinds of sonorities does the coincidence of the rows create?
3. Study measures 1-13. Again four statements of the row are used. Measures 6-7 represent an overlapping of the four rows with another set of four rows. Trace the use of the row in these opening thirteen measures.
4. The overlapping of rows is continued in measures 19-20 and throughout the rest of the piece. Trace the row throughout the movement.
5. How do the melodic lines and sonorities reflect the row?
6. Analyze elements of repetition and return. What chords, motives, timbres, etc. are reused?
7. How do rhythm and texture contribute to form?
8. How do spacing and octave displacement create contrast? What effect do dynamic levels have on this composition?

OTHER WORKS TO STUDY

Webern, Anton: *Five Pieces for String Quartet,* Op. 5 (1909)
Symphony, Op. 21 (1928)
Boulez, Pierre: *Le Marteau sans maître* (1955)
Stockhausen, Karlheinz: *Klavierstücke* (1954-1961)

ANTON WEBERN

Cantata, Op. 29

FIRST MOVEMENT

rit.
getragen
Fl.
Ob.
Kl.
Bass-Kl.
Hr.
Trp.
Pos.
Hrf.
Cel.
Pk.
gr. Tr.
Sopr.
Alt
Ten.
Bass
1. Gg.
2. Gg.
Alle
Br.
Vlc.

lebhaft
getragen
lebhaft
getragen
rit. - - -
8
9
10
11
12
Fl.
Ob.
Kl.
Bass-Kl.
Hr.
Trp.
Pos.
Hrf.
Cel.
Pk.
gr.Tr.
Sopr.
Alt
Ten.
Bass
lebhaft
getragen
lebhaft
getragen
rit. - - -
Alle
Solo
Dpf. ab
Solo pizz.
Alle arco
Dpf. ab
Solo
1.Gg.
2.Gg.
Br.
Vlc.
lebhaft
getragen
lebhaft
getragen
rit. - - -
8
9
10
11
12

lebhaft
13
14
15
16
getragen
17
Fl.
Ob.
Kl.
Bass-Kl.
Hr.
Trp.
Pos.
sff
Hrf.
Cel.
Pk.
mit 2 Tellern
ff
Bk.
Sopr.
Zün - den - der
Light - ning, the
Licht - blitz
kind - ler
des
of
Le - - bens
Be - - ing,
Alt
Ten.
Zün - den - der
Light - ning, the
Licht - blitz
kind - ler
des
of
Le - - bens
Be - - ing,
Bass
1.Gg.
2.Gg.
Br.
Dpf. ab
Vlc.
Dpf. ab

lebhaft
getragen
lebhaft
Fl.
Ob.
Kl.
Bass-Kl.
Hr.
Trp.
Pos.
Hrf.
Cel.
Pk.
Schlgwk
Sopr.
schlug
struck,
ein
flashed
aus der Wol - ke des Wor - tes.
from the word in the storm cloud.
Alt
Ten.
schlug
struck,
ein
flashed
aus der Wol - ke des Wor - tes.
from the word in the storm cloud.
Bass
lebhaft
o.Dpf. Alle
pizz.
getragen
lebhaft
1.Gg.
2.Gg.
o.Dpf. pizz.
o.Dpf. pizz.
Br.
o.Dpf. Alle pizz.
Vlc.
lebhaft
getragen
lebhaft

getragen
lebhaft
getragen
lebhaft
23
24
25
26
27
Fl.
Ob.
Kl.
Bass-Kl.
Hr.
mit Dpf.
Trp.
molto f
Pos.
molto f
Hrf.
Cel.
Pk.
gr. Tr.
Bk.
Sopr.
Don - ner
Thun - der,
der
the
Alt
Ten.
Don - ner
Thun - der,
der
the
Bass
getragen
lebhaft
getragen
lebhaft
1.Gg.
arco G-Saite
molto f
pizz.
2.Gg.
pizz.
Dpf. auf
Br.
pizz.
Dpf. auf
Vlc.
arco
molto f
pizz.
getragen
lebhaft
getragen
lebhaft
23
24
25
26
27
molto f
molto f
molto f

getragen
28
lebhaft
29
getragen
30
lebhaft
31
rit.
Fl.
Ob.
Kl.
Bass-Kl.
Hr.
m. Dpf.
Dpf. ab
Trp.
Pos.
Hrf.
Cel.
Pk.
Bk.
Sopr.
Herz - schlag
heart beat,
folgt nach,
fol - lows,
Alt
Ten.
Herz - schlag
heart beat,
folgt nach,
fol - lows,
Bass
getragen
lebhaft
getragen
Solo
arco
Alle
lebhaft
rit.
1.Gg.
2.Gg.
Br.
arco
Solo
Vlc.
getragen
28
lebhaft
29
getragen
30
lebhaft
31
rit.

getragen
lebhaft
getragen
rit. - - -
lebhaft
Fl.
Ob.
Kl.
Bass-Kl.
Hr.
Trp.
Pos.
Hrf.
Cel.
Pk.
Schlgwk
Sopr.
bis er in Frie - den ver - ebbt.
at last dis - solv - ing in peace.
Alt
Ten.
bis er in Frie - den ver - ebbt.
at last dis - solv - ing in peace.
Bass
Dpf. auf
I.Gg.
2.Gg.
Br.
Dpf. auf
Vlc.

getragen
37
lebhaft
rit. - - -
38
tempo
39
getragen
40
lebhaft
rit. - - -
41
Fl.
Ob.
Kl.
Bass-Kl.
Hr.
Trp.
Pos.
Hrf.
Cel.
Pk.
Schlgwk.
Sopr.
Alt
Ten.
Bass
ohne Dpf.
Dpf. auf
molto f
1. Gg.
2. Gg.
Br.
Vlc.
m. Dpf.
mit Dpf.
pizz.
Solo
arco
Alle
mit Dpf.
Alle

tempo
getragen
lebhaft
rit.
tempo
rit.
getragen
rit.
Fl.
Ob.
Kl.
Bass-Kl.
Hr.
Trp.
Pos.
Hrf.
Cel.
gr.Tr.
Bk.
Trgl.
Sopr.
Alt
Ten.
Bass
mit Dpf.
1.Gg.
2.Gg.
Br.
Vlc.
arco
molto f
pizz.
Solo
Alle

List of Compositions Chronologically

Date	Composer	Composition
1906-1910	Ives, Charles	*Second Sonata for Violin and Piano*
1908-1909	Berg, Alban	*Four Songs,* Op. 2
1909	Webern, Anton	*Six Pieces for Orchestra,* Op. 6
1911	Schoenberg, Arnold	*Six Short Pieces for Piano,* Op. 19
1911	Stravinsky, Igor	*Petroushka*
1918	Stravinsky, Igor	*L'Histoire du Soldat*
1921	Berg, Alban	*Wozzeck*
1923	Hindemith, Paul	*String Quartet,* Op. 22
1925	Schoenberg, Arnold	*Suite for Piano,* Op. 25
1928	Schoenberg, Arnold	*Variations for Orchestra,* Op. 31
1926-1937	Bartók, Béla	*Mikrokosmos*
1931	Bartók, Béla	*Forty-Four Violin Duets*
1939	Bartók, Béla	*Sixth Quartet*
1940	Webern, Anton	*Cantata,* Op. 29
1942	Hindemith, Paul	*Ludus Tonalis*
1943-1945	Copland, Aaron	*Appalachian Spring*
1950	Carter, Elliott	*Eight Etudes and a Fantasy for Woodwind Quartet*
1950	Persichetti, Vincent	*Divertimento for Band*
1954	Stravinsky, Igor	*In Memoriam Dylan Thomas*
1955	Stravinsky, Igor	*Canticum Sacrum*
1959	Powell, Mel	*Filigree Setting for String Quartet*
1959	Schuller, Gunther	*Seven Studies on Themes of Paul Klee*
1967	Gaburo, Kenneth	*Antiphony IV*

List of Compositions by Medium

Medium	Composition	Composer
Band	*Divertimento for Band*	Vincent Persichetti
Chamber ensemble	*Antiphony IV*	Kenneth Gaburo
	L'Histoire du Soldat	Igor Stravinsky
	In Memoriam Dylan Thomas	Igor Stravinsky
Orchestra	*Appalachian Spring*	Aaron Copland
	Variations for Orchestra, Op. 31	Arnold Schoenberg
	Seven Studies on Themes of Paul Klee	Gunther Schuller
	Petroushka	Igor Stravinsky
	Six Pieces for Orchestra, Op. 6	Anton Webern
Piano	*Mikrokosmos*	Béla Bartók
	Ludus Tonalis	Paul Hindemith
	Six Short Pieces for Piano, Op. 19	Arnold Schoenberg
	Suite for Piano, Op. 25	Arnold Schoenberg
String ensemble	*Sixth Quartet*	Béla Bartók
	Forty-Four Violin Duets	Béla Bartók
	String Quartet, Op. 22	Paul Hindemith
	Second Sonata for Violin and Piano	Charles Ives
	Filigree Setting for String Quartet	Mel Powell
Vocal	*Four Songs,* Op. 2	Alban Berg
	Wozzeck	Alban Berg
	Canticum Sacrum	Igor Stravinsky
	Cantata, Op. 29	Anton Webern
Woodwind	*Eight Etudes and a Fantasy for Woodwind Quartet*	Elliott Carter

List of Composers' Dates

Composer	Dates
Schoenberg, Arnold	1874-1951
Ives, Charles	1874-1954
Bartók, Béla	1881-1945
Stravinsky, Igor	1882-
Webern, Anton	1883-1945
Berg, Alban	1885-1935
Hindemith, Paul	1895-1963
Copland, Aaron	1900-
Carter, Elliott	1908-
Persichetti, Vincent	1915-
Powell, Mel	1923-
Schuller, Gunther	1925-
Gaburo, Kenneth	1926-

Selected List of Recordings

Bartók, Béla. *Mikrokosmos* (complete), Vox SVBX-5425 (Sándor)
Duos for Two Violins, Bartók 907 (Ajtay, Kuttner)
Angel S-36360 (Menuhin, Gotkovsky)
String Quartets (complete), Concert-Disc 501 (207/9) (Fine Arts Quartet)
Columbia D3S-717 (Juilliard Quartet)

Berg, Alban. *Four Songs,* Op. 2, Angel S-36480 (Harper)
Lyrichord 94 (Rowe)
Wozzeck (complete), Deutsche Grammophon Gesellschaft 138991/2
Columbia SL-118

Carter, Elliott. *Eight Etudes and a Fantasy for Woodwind Quartet,* Concert-Disc 229
(New York Woodwind Quartet)

Copland, Aaron. *Appalachian Spring,* Columbia ML-5157 (Philadelphia Orchestra)
Columbia MS-6355 (New York Philharmonic Orchestra)
RCA Victor LSC-2401 (Boston Symphony Orchestra)

Gaburo, Kenneth. *Antiphony IV,* Nonesuch 71199 (University of Illinois Contemporary Chamber Players)

Hindemith, Paul. *Quartet,* Op. 22, Concert-Disc 225 (Fine Arts Quartet)
Ludus Tonalis, Philips 900-096 (Laretei)

Ives, Charles. *Sonatas for Violin and Piano* (complete), Philips World Series s-2-002 (Druian, Simms)

Persichetti, Vincent. *Divertimento for Band,* Mercury 50079 (Eastman Symphonic Wind Ensemble)

Powell, Mel. *Filigree Setting,* Son-Nova 1 (Claremont String Quartet)

Schoenberg, Arnold. *Piano Music,* Op. 19 and Op. 25, Columbia MS-7098 (Gould)
Variations for Orchestra, Op. 31, Columbia M2S-694 (CBC Symphony)

Schuller, Gunther. *Seven Studies on Themes of Paul Klee,* RCA Victor LSC-2879 (Boston Symphony Orchestra)
Mercury MG50282 (Minneapolis Symphony)

Stravinsky, Igor. *Petroushka,* Columbia MS-6332 (Columbia Symphony)
RCA Victor LSC-2376 (Boston Symphony)
L'Histoire du Soldat, Columbia MS-6272 (Columbia Symphony)
In Memoriam Dylan Thomas, Columbia MS-6992 (Columbia Chamber Ensemble)
Canticum Sacrum, Columbia CMS-6022

Webern, Anton. *Complete Works,* Columbia CK4L-232
Cantata, Op. 29, Angel S-36480
Nonesuch 71192
Six Pieces for Orchestra, Op. 6, Columbia MS-6216 (Columbia Symphony)